Born in Crisis
and
Shaped by Controversy

Born in Crisis
and
Shaped by Controversy

The Relevant History of Methodism

Volume 2
Shaped by Controversy

JOHN R. TYSON

 CASCADE *Books* • Eugene, Oregon

BORN IN CRISIS AND SHAPED BY CONTROVERSY
The Relevant History of Methodism, Volume 2: Shaped by Controversy

Cascade Books
An Imprint of Wipf and Stock Publishers
199 W. 8th Ave., Suite 3
Eugene, OR 97401

www.wipfandstock.com

PAPERBACK ISBN: 978-1-6667-3725-7
HARDCOVER ISBN: 978-1-6667-3726-4
EBOOK ISBN: 978-1-6667-3727-1

Cataloguing-in-Publication data:

Names: Tyson, John R., author.

Title: Born in crisis and shaped by controversy : the relevant history of methodism,
   volume 2 : shaped by controversy / John R. Tyson.

Description: Eugene, OR : Cascade Books, 2023 | Includes bibliographical references
   and index.

Identifiers: ISBN 978-1-6667-3725-7 (paperback) | ISBN 978-1-6667-3726-4 (hardcover)
   | ISBN 978-1-6667-3727-1 (ebook)

Subjects: LCSH: Methodism—History—18th century. | Methodism—History—19th
   century. | Methodism—History—20th century. | Methodism—History—21st century.

Classification: BX8231 .T97 2023 (paperback) | BX8231 .T97 (ebook)

VERSION NUMBER 072023

Contents

Preface

THIS VOLUME IS THE second installment of *Born in Crisis and Shaped by Controversy: The Relevant History of Methodism*. Where *Born in Crisis* explored the religious, social, and economic crisis that birthed Methodism, *Shaped by Controversy* follows Methodism through the growing pains and controversies that occurred as the Methodist movement became the Methodist Church, and then very soon the many Methodist churches. If for some reason you have missed the first part of this study, which described how Methodism was *Born in Crisis*, you can still easily and productively ride along with this train of thought—even though you are getting on board at the first stop or midpoint.

I want to thank the clergy and laity who participated in various parts of this journey with me through one of the several retreats at Camp Asbury, Casowasco, and Sky Lake, or the "district days," hosted by the Binghamton, Cornerstone, and Northern Flow UMC Districts, where some of these ideas were road-tested in broad terms. I am grateful to my colleagues who took classes at Colgate Rochester Crozer Divinity School, and the UMC Course of Study where many of these inquiries were born, examined, and discussed. I appreciate the wonderful opportunity given me by the clergy and laity of Asbury First UMC, Covenant UMC, and Webster UMC, all in Rochester, New York, to walk through several of these crises and controversies in conversation with them. And finally, I am deeply indebted to friends and colleagues in ministry who read, discussed, and helped me improve various sections of this manuscript. Among these are: Rev. Hannah Bonner, Dr. Richard Hays, Dr. Ann Kemper, Rev. Rick La Due, Ms. Pat Lunn, Dr. Marvin McMickle, Dr. Angela Sims, Dr. Hilary Jerome Scarcella, and many others who I might have forgotten. Obviously, however, the opinions, judgments, and shortcomings herein are entirely my own.

Introduction

THE METHODIST MOVEMENT WAS "born in crisis" or actually a powerful and sometimes pernicious collection of crises; this was the premise and the point of the first volume in this sequence, *Born in Crisis*. In many ways, the Wesleys' and early Methodists' willingness to acknowledge and seek to address these crises contributed significantly to the making and the shaping of early Methodism. Being or trying to be faithful Christian witnesses and stewards in the midst of these challenges helped define Methodists as a people who pursued personal and social holiness because, following John Wesley's "prime directive," they intended to "reform the nation, particularly the Church; and to spread scriptural holiness over the land."[1]

Family history matters. How many of us have plugged into Ancestry. com to find out about who we are by tracing our DNA, our relationships, locations, and relocations, our family's history or many histories? It helps us get a pretty good idea of who we were and where we came from as a part of understanding who we are and what we are about. In some sense we are looking for what's hardwired "into" us by the journey from the past to where we are today; the same is true (to some degree) about looking into the history of our ecclesiastical family. But the inner dynamics of our "family systems" matter too, sometimes they matter *a lot*. Consciously, but often unconsciously, intrafamily conflicts and controversy have shaped each of us in lasting ways. In a similar way, the Methodist family has come through many struggles and significant trauma that have shaped our identity.

The first half of this study showed us that Methodists were, from their very inception of the movement, people who were able to discern the danger of using religion to buttress political policies. They were people who sought to find a balance place between Christian faith and a common-sense use of reason. The early Methodists wanted to shake themselves and others out of the comfort zone of ecclesiastical lethargy and inaction. They were

---

1. Wesley, *Works of John Wesley*, VIII, "Large Minutes," 299.

people who were sensitive to the immoral use of social privileges that the few could and should use to help the many. They were well aware of the pain of poverty and the exploitation that often accompanies economic disparity and they understood and sought to alleviate the hopelessness of people who kept working harder and harder and kept getting poorer and poorer. The early Methodists valued, enabled, and elevated women at a time when society excluded them. They embraced the equality of all people, including people of African descent, and joined the crusade for their social and political equality. They were scandalized by hateful rhetoric and actions that were wrapped in religious garb and pointed out the atrocities it caused. And they celebrated the peace, joy, and happiness that is found in God through Christ, and pursued it in ways that were consistent with a robust understanding of their lives as vehicles for Christian stewardship.

This second installment of the Methodist story, *Shaped by Controversy*, examines eight major controversies that epitomize crucial elements of Methodism's interfamily dialogue and trauma. These theological, ecclesial, and ethical controversies tried values, tested patience, and strained familial relationships; ultimately they divided the Methodist movement. Ironically, as we shall see below, quite often these controversies were rooted in something that was good and right about the Methodist movement or Christian faith, which somehow got out of balance and became destructive; things like waiting upon the Lord, trusting in God's powerful and inscrutable will, or striving for holiness of heart and life. The internal struggles over matters related to class, economic status, gender, and race shook Methodism precisely because the inclusion of all people from diverse backgrounds and walks of life was a formative part of the early Methodist movement.

These contentious controversies revolved around matters like: 1) the nature of spiritual life, faith, and good works; 2) predestination and the nature of Christian assurance of salvation; 3) the difficulties of living out Christian perfection in a world full of imperfect people; 4) the pain and trauma of ecclesiastical separation; 5) controversies over women's leadership; 6) the debilitating effects of racism and segregation; 7) controversy over institutional governance and shared leadership; and 8) conflict over the affirmation and full inclusion of LGBTQ people. These controversies within "the family" have challenged and pained Methodists deeply. These issues have also forced Methodists to examine their priorities and clarify what matters most to them. How the Methodists responded to these controversies, for good or for ill, has shaped the identity of the Methodists as people of faith. On several occasions interfamily strife has led to painful separations, and divisions among Christian friends, colleagues, churches, and institutions. Since once again, now in the twenty-first century, a segment of the Methodist family has come to the point of schism due to controversy over the full inclusion of queer people, this is a very appropriate time to take another look at the controversial character of Methodism's "family story." In each case, however, there are lessons to be learned about the ongoing challenges of vital piety, wealth, power, acceptance, and prejudice, and the temptations of respectability, institutional growth, or survival; with that in mind, each of these controversies is explored in a chapter that follows. Hopefully, we can find in this history both guidance and encouragement because our past is often like a distant mirror that reflects very clearly upon our lives today.

Sir Winston Churchill is reputed to have said: "history is written by the victors." Whether the attribution is entirely accurate or not, the assessment certainly is. The resources available and terminology developed to chronicle any history—including the current one—have been dramatically shaped by the invisible hands and minds of those celebrating their "victories." This means that some of the most challenging of the Methodist controversies have been recorded and told in terms that remain hurtful to those who have been harmed by that history. For example, the paper trail that is available to chart the course of Methodism's engagement with issues like the equality and inclusion of women, people of color, and LGBTQ people has been recorded in tones already tainted by patriarchy, racism, and white supremacy, as well as binary and oppositional approaches to understanding gender and human sexual expression. And to that degree, the very way in which the story has been told—even in our attempts to tell it well and to analyze and critique it—becomes still another instance of hurt and harm. For this reason, it seems very difficult to reframe the Methodist story in ways that do not participate in and perpetuate this situation. But perhaps acknowledging and naming this part of the problem is a first step in the task of trying to reshape the telling of our family story in ways and terms that do not imply that prejudice, poverty, classism, will-to-power, chauvinism, racism, and homophobia are acceptable social norms for Christians, or for Methodists.

For good and for ill, these many events and challenges have shaped our lives together as Methodists, and they have become a part of our collective history. The exploration of what was at stake in each of these crises and controversies reminds us who we are, and helps us reexamine our values and priories. This examination bids us to develop ways and resources to meet the challenges of our own crises and approaches to resolve conflict among us. At basis, then, this is a story of hope and instruction. It reminds us how long and how strong God's presence has been among us. Crises have been faced, and challenges have been overcome; and this has been a source of joy and relief. There have been many sad and frustrating aspects to the

Methodist story as well; mistakes have been made, and we need to try to learn to grow from them. Because of the joys as well as the challenges of our complicated family history, John Wesley's dying words ring true to me, as "the people called Methodists" look forward to an uncertain future: "best of all, God is with us."[2]

---

2. Wesley, *Journal of Rev. John Wesley*, VIII:143.

CHAPTER 11

"Swallowed up in a Sea of Stillness"
Controversy over Faith and Good Works

THE FIRST INTERNAL CONTROVERSY that shook and then divided the infant Methodist movement was born out of an excessive emphasis upon a very good thing—the cultivation of a vital inner life. The Wesley brothers described the situation in the preface to their *Hymns and Sacred Poems* (1739), where they acknowledged that earlier in their own Christian journey they had pursued God's acceptance largely through the performance of religious duties and good works. As they studied and matured, they followed "the scheme of the Mystic divines," which at the time was very helpful to the Wesleys, since "they speak largely and well against expecting to be accepted of God for our virtuous actions; and then teach, that we are to be accepted for our virtuous habits or tempers."[1] And yet, looking back from the perspective of the grace-filled experiences of God's acceptance, Charles and then John had found, in May 1738, when they embraced justification by faith in Christ as the sole basis of their acceptance before God, the guidance of those "mystical divines" deficient because "still the ground of our acceptance [by God] is placed in *ourselves*."[2]

The Wesleys' experience of God's free grace and acceptance received by living faith in Christ changed their understanding of Christian faith. The reformation doctrine of justification by faith alone was introduced to them through the writings of Martin Luther as mediated to them through the Moravians. Justification, acceptance, and approval by God they came to see

1. C. Wesley and J. Wesley, *Poetical Works*, I:ix.
2. C. Wesley and J. Wesley, *Poetical Works*, I:ix, emphasis added.

was by grace, for "by grace are ye saved through faith; and that not of your-selves: it is the gift of God" (Eph 2:8): a divine gift, not a human endeavor.

Although the Wesleys sometimes wrote or spoke as though they never really had "faith" prior to their conversions, in truth however, what they really discovered that May was a *different* kind of faith. Their discovery brought with it a new understanding of the respective roles that faith and good works play in Christian life. Charles explained the situation to their mystical mentor, William Law, in this way: "I told him, he was my school-master to bring me to Christ; but the reason why I did not come sooner to Him, was my seeking to be sanctified before I was justified."[3] Said simply, holy living (i.e., sanctification) flows from one's acceptance and renewal by God through faith in Jesus Christ (i.e., justification); holiness was the *result* of saving faith, *not* the cause of it. John Wesley made the same point by distinguishing between what he described as "the faith of a servant" and "the faith of a child of God." "Fifty years ago," Wesley recalled, "the preach-ers commonly called Methodists began to preach that grand scriptural doctrine, salvation by faith, they were not sufficiently appraised of the dif-ference between a servant and a child of God."[4] The "servant" reverences God and serves God out of duty and holy obligation; but "the child of God" understands themself as a beloved member of God's family. Their accep-tance by God is bestowed upon them because of their familial relationship, it does not need to be earned. Because of that relationship with God, they have a profound inner sense of God's acceptance, and the joy and gratitude of feeling "at home" with God. John explained:

> the faith of a child is properly and directly a divine conviction whereby every child of God is enabled to testify, "the life that I now live, I live by faith in the Son of God, who loved me, and gave himself for me." And whosoever hath this, "the Spirit of God witnesses with his spirit that he is a child of God." . . . "And because ye are sons, God hath sent forth the Spirit of the Son into your hearts, crying, 'Abba Father;' that is, giving you a childlike confidence in him, together with a kind affection toward him."[5]

The Wesleys saw a second flaw in their earlier reliance upon "the mys-tic divines"; "they advise 'to the desert, to the desert, and God will build you up,'" they recalled.[6] This approach implied a passivity in the life of faith that seemed improper to John and Charles. And it still made oneself the focus of

3. C. Wesley, *Manuscript Journal*, I:184.

4. J. Wesley, "On Faith," in *Sermons*, III:497.

5. J. Wesley, "On Faith," in *Sermons*, III:498.

6. C. Wesley and J. Wesley, *Poetical Works*, I:xx.

one's concern, not the needs or fellowship of others. This sort of "mysticism," they believed, was still another variety of self-centered living, one that was dressed up in religious garb, but did not honor the self-giving gospel of Jesus Christ. As the Wesleys' preface further explained: "The religion these authors would edify us in is solitary religion. If thou will be perfect, say they, 'trouble not thyself about outward works. It is better to work virtues in the will.'"[7] The Wesleys considered the mystical emphasis upon withdrawal from the world in order to cultivate inner virtues to be utterly foreign to the gospel of Christ. "'Holy solitaries,'" John wrote, "is a phrase no more consistent with the Gospel than 'holy adulterers.' The Gospel of Christ knows of no religion, but social; no holiness, but social holiness. Faith working by love is the length and breadth and depth and height of Christian Perfection."[8] While "the mystic divines" offered course correction to the Wesleys' earlier emphasis upon external duties, they also came to believe that the inwardness, individualism, and the holy inaction of the mystics were significant errors.

Johann Valentin Haidt, *English Moravians in an Audience with King George II* (circa. 1752–54), oil on canvas, located at the National Portrait Gallery, London. From Wikimedia (public domain).

As a corrective to the danger of being "holy solitaries," the Wesley brothers participated in small groups and instituted the "classes" and

7. C. Wesley and J. Wesley, *Poetical Works*, I:xxii.
8. C. Wesley and J. Wesley, *Poetical Works*, I:xxii.

"bands" that formed the infrastructure of Methodist movement. They were working out the balance point between inner and outer holiness, faith and good works, at precisely the same time a controversy erupted between the Wesley brothers and their friends, the English Moravians. John and Charles first met Moravians during their Georgia mission, and felt a deep spiritual kinship with them. Moravian missionaries like Nicholas Zinzendorf (1700–1760), and Peter Böhler (1712–75), bishops of the *Unitas Fratum* (United Brothers) or Moravian Church, had been instrumental in the Wesleys' process of clarifying the nature of saving faith. When they returned to London, the Wesleys, along with Howel Harris, James Hutton, Peter Böhler (all Moravians), and others participated in the close Christian fellowship of a small group called the Fetter Lane Society.

The Wesley brothers joined the Fetter Lane Society after their conversion experiences through their acquaintance with many of the principal members. At that time, it was an interfaith group with Anglicans and English Moravians fellowshiping together, and the Wesleys formed friendships and spiritual alliances with several Moravians. In less than a year, however, tensions began to emerge among participants of the Fetter Lane Society as some of the Moravians began to practice a quietism, or "stillness," that eschewed all good works. It was an extreme expression of the belief in "justification by faith *alone*," which led some members of the group to avoid good works entirely in order to ensure they were not *trusting* works as the means of their salvation.[9] The dilemma was complicated by the interfaith identity of the group, and its rather informal approach to leadership.

John's and Charles's journals traced the emergence of the radical quietism in the Fetter Lane Society to the arrival of Phillip Molther, a Moravian missionary who arrived from Germany in October 1739. But Colin Podmore's research indicates that by April of 1739, members of the Fetter Lane Society already considered themselves so "saved" that they felt free to neglect prayer, Bible reading, and even communion; James Hutton, Howel Harris, and John Bray were among the principal people behind this spiritual development.[10] Since the Wesleys were sporadic in their attendance at Fetter Lane, due to their itinerant preaching engagements, it is likely that these developments began in their absence. Since the Fetter Lane Society was dedicated to the serious pursuit of Christian holiness and spiritual growth, a fundamental difference of opinion on *how* best to pursue that goal became very challenging.

9. Podmore, *Moravian Church in England*, 60–61. Emphasis original.

10. Podmore, *Moravian Church in England*, 61.

Soon after his arrival in London, Phillip Molther visited the Fetter Lane Society and was shocked by the groaning, crying out, contortions, and other strange gestures that erupted during worship there. It was "enough to bring one out in a cold sweat," he confided to a colleague.[11] Molther, likely in reaction to the ruckus he witnessed in mid-October, stressed the importance of introspection, prayer, and waiting before the Lord in deep introspection. He pointed to Scriptures like "Be still and know that I am God" (Ps 46:10), and urged his colleagues to be like the first disciples and "not depart from Jerusalem, but wait for the promise of the Father, which, saith he, ye have heard of me" (Acts 1:4). He saw that verse as indicting a passive, reflective spirituality, along with meditative waiting for the immediate leading of God the Holy Spirit. This interpretation fit well the cardinal doctrine of "justification by faith alone," which the Moravians had inherited from Martin Luther and subsequently shared with the Wesleys. The "alone" aspect ruled out the contribution of human good works to the process of salvation. Molther's passive spirituality must have seemed to be a valid expression of Christian mysticism, because many others in the Fetter Lane Society, perhaps including Charles Wesley, embraced it for a time. Selina Hastings, the Countess of Huntingdon, sent a news report to John Wesley while he was on the road:

> Since you left us the Still Ones are not without their attacks. I fear much more for him [Charles Wesley] than myself. . . . They have by one of their agents pressed me very much to see Spannenberg, but I have taken no sort of notice as if I had not heard it. I comfort myself very much that you will approve of a step with respect to them your brother and I have taken! No less than his declaring open war against them. He seemed under some difficulty about it at first, till he had free liberty given him to use my name as the instrument of God's hand that had delivered him from them.[12]

The "stillness" spirituality seemed excessive and wrong to the Wesleys and Lady Huntingdon, and this disagreement put them on a collision course with several of their Christian friends and allies.

If this disagreement could have been settled by a simple appeal to the words of Scripture, a resolution among Bible-believing Christians would have been, if not easy, at least possible. But Scripture passages could be cited on both sides of the argument: to Molther's "Be still and know I am God" (Ps 46:10), the Wesleys could have replied, "Faith without works is dead"

11. Podmore, *Moravian Church in England*, 59.

12. Lady Huntingdon, "Letter to John Wesley, Oct. 24, 1741," quoted in Tyson and Schlenther, *In the Midst of Early Methodism*, 48–49.

(Jas 2:20), or cited Jesus' eucharistic command, "*Do this* in remembrance of me" (Luke 22:19). The controversy was further complicated by the fact that it was a contention among Christian friends.

The "stillness controversy" that began in Fetter Lane quickly spread into the Methodist movement because several people participated in both groups, and that development escalated its importance significantly. On November 4, 1739, John Wesley found the Methodist Society in London had turned into a quiet Quaker meeting: "Our society met at seven in the morning," he wrote, "and continued *silent* till eight. One then spoke of 'looking unto Jesus' and exhorted us all 'to lie *still* in his hand.'"[13] On that same evening, John met a second, equally disturbing event: "Some of our brethren strongly intimated that none of them had any true faith; and that asserted in plain terms (1) that till they had true faith, they ought to be *still*, that is . . . 'to abstain from the means of grace, as they are called—the Lord's Supper *in particular*'; (2) that '*the ordinances are not means of grace,* there being no other means than Christ.'"[14] John was deeply distressed by these views but was not able to counteract them. At the next meeting, John Wesley found the group convulsed by controversy: "I found every day the dreadful effects of our brethren's reasonings, and disputing with each other. Scarce one in ten retained his first love, and most of the rest were in the utmost confusion, biting and devouring one another."[15]

On December 31, 1739, John had "a long and particular conversation with Mr. Molther himself," and wrote up a three-page summary "of the difference between us," in he which blamed the whole matter on John Molther's innovations. The crux of the matter, as Wesley saw it, was threefold: (1) Molther understood faith to be entirely passive on the part of the believer, whereas the Methodists understood faith to be a cooperative event between God and humans; (2) Mothler urged people to wait in stillness until they receive faith in its fullest expression; (3) this "waiting" excluded the use of any of the spiritual disciplines the Methodists had come to cherish, because (according to Molther) it was not possible for a person to use the means of grace without "trusting in them," and one should trust in Christ alone.[16] By January 3, 1740, Wesley was back on the road again, as he "endeavored to explain to our brethren the true, Christian, scriptural *stillness*."[17] That same

---

13. J. Wesley, *Journal and Diaries*, II:119–20. Emphasis original.

14. J. Wesley, *Journal and Diaries*, II:119–20. Emphasis original.

15. J. Wesley, *Journal and Diaries*, II:130.

16. J. Wesley, *Journal and Diaries*, II:131–34.

17. J. Wesley, *Journal and Diaries*, II:134. Emphasis original.

spring, Charles Wesley encountered the stillness spirituality among friends and former colleagues like "poor perverted Mr. Simpson." Charles wrote:

> I asked whether he was *still* in the means of grace, or *out* of them. "Means of grace!" he answered; "there are none. Neither is there any good to be got by those you call such, or any obligation to use them. . . . Most of us have cast them off. You must not speak a word in recommendation of them; that is setting people upon working [out their salvation]."[18]

By the summer of 1740, it was clear several months of contention had resolved nothing and had forced almost everyone in Methodism to choose sides. So in June of 1740, John and Charles Wesley agreed to a "new-modeling of the bands," saving those who were "still for the ordinances" from the criticism and rancor of the others who were not.[19] Charles reported, "We gathered up our wreck . . . nine out of ten are swallowed up in the dead sea of stillness. Oh, why was this not done six months ago? How fatal was our delay and false moderation!"[20] Famous for his plain speaking, on his way out the door Charles served up a parting shot: "I told them plainly, I *should only continue with them so long as they continued in the Church of England.* My every word was grievous to them. I am a thorn in their sides, and they cannot bear me."[21] Charles rightly understood the stillness practices as antithetical to those of the Church of England.

The Stillness Controversy led to the first schism in the infant Methodist movement. It was more than a theoretical debate, it was like a divorce in the family because former friends and colleagues parted ways. Both sides seemed to have the Bible on their side, and both sought to defend what they understood to be crucial Christian truths; justification by faith *alone*, on the one hand, and the importance the Lord's Supper, spiritual disciples, and other "good works" on the other. These were matters that seemed too important for Christian faith and practice for either side to simply paper over their differences, or as the Wesleys would say in the midst of a later controversy, "to agree to disagree."

Part of this controversial schism over faith and works was also about the Methodists' Anglican roots. Where the Moravians followed and perhaps radicalized Martin Luther's formulation of justification by faith *alone*, the Wesleys moderated that view of justification by faith with the Church of England's belief that saving faith is "a faith that worketh by love" (Gal 5:6).

18. C. Wesley, *Manuscript Journal*, I:232. Emphasis original.

19. C. Wesley, *Manuscript Journal*, I:267.

20. C. Wesley, *Manuscript Journal*, I:267.

21. C. Wesley, *Manuscript Journal*, I:268. Emphasis original.

This "True and Lively Faith" was explained in the Anglican Standard Homily no. 4, by that same title:

> Of this faith three things are specially to be noted; first, that this
> faith doth not lie dead in the heart, but is lively and fruitful in
> bringing forth good works; second, that without it can no good
> works be done that shall be acceptable and pleasant to God;
> third, what manner of good works they be that this faith doth
> bring forth.[22]

This understanding of the relationship of faith and good works meant that in the Anglican and Wesleyan views, salvation is a cooperative event, which John explained so well in his sermon "On Working Out Our Own Salvation." Based on Philippians 2:12–13, John described the process of salvation as our cooperating with God, while God was already at work within us. And since salvation is comprised of two parts, justification ("what God does *for us*") and sanctification ("what God does *in us*"), it is appropriate to say that while justification comes through faith alone, our sanctification also requires that we cooperate with God's grace.[23] Hence, the Methodist understanding of "The Scripture Way of Salvation" embraced justification by faith, as well as works of piety "such as public prayer, family prayer, and praying in our closet; receiving the Supper of the Lord; searching the Scriptures by hearing, reading, meditating; and using such a measure of fasting or abstinence as our bodily health allows" as well as "works of mercy—such as feeding the hungry, clothing the naked, entertaining the stranger, visiting those that are in prison, or sick, or variously afflicted."[24]

The Stillness Controversy helped the Methodists to try to steer a middle course between those "who abused the ordinances of God" by their incessant but empty repetition, and those "who despised" the ordinances by not using them all.[25] Good works, that is, works of piety (spiritual disciplines) and works of mercy (humanitarian service), do not justify a person or earn their acceptance by God, but the faith that saves is "a faith that worketh by love"—a faith that grows by exercising in love for God and God's people.

The Stillness Controversy forced the Methodists to explain more clearly what they meant by the "means of grace." John wrote, "I understand outward signs, words, or actions ordained of God, and appointed for this end—to be the *ordinary* channels whereby he might convey to men

---

22. *Book of Homilies*, 32.
23. J. Wesley, *Sermons*, II:157–58, 163–64.
24. J. Wesley, *Sermons*, II:166.
25. J. Wesley, *Sermons*, I:379.

preventing, justifying, or sanctifying grace."[26] John Wesley's sermon "The Means of Grace" (1746) reflected his debate with Phillip Molther without actually mentioning it: "The expression some have used, 'Christ is the only means of grace' does not exclude the use of these spiritual disciplines, because Christ commanded it and Christ meets the seeker in and through them; hence, the grace or salvation received properly comes only through faith in Jesus Christ," but it comes to us through "the ordinary channels" of spiritual discipline God has "appointed for this end."[27] One wonders if John Wesley had said in 1739 what he wrote so clearly in 1746 whether the controversy would have been so rancorous.

The Stillness Controversy also caused the Methodists to clarify their theology of the Lord's Supper, and in what sense communion is a "means of grace." In 1738–39, Charles wrote a twenty-three-verse hymn to explain the topic, and it was soon followed by an entire volume of *Hymns on the Lord's Supper* (1745). In his "Eucharist Hymn, XXVIII," Charles explained that while Christ is our only means of grace, we can meet Christ in the Eucharist and thereby receive his grace by faith. The Lord's Supper is, in that sense, both "a sign and means of grace":

> Author of our salvation, Thee
> With lowly thankful hearts we praise,
> Author of this great mystery,
> Figure and means of saving grace.
>
> The sacred, true, effectual sign,
> Thy body and Thy blood it shows;
> The glorious instrument Divine
> Thy mercy and Thy strength bestows.
>
> We see the blood that seals our peace,
> Thy pardoning mercy we receive;
> The bread doth visibly express
> The strength through which our spirits live.
>
> Our spirits drink a fresh supply,
> And eat the bread so freely given,
> Till borne on eagle's wings we fly,
> And banquet with our Lord in heaven.[28]

---

26. J. Wesley, *Sermons*, I:381. Emphasis original.
27. J. Wesley, *Sermons*, I:382.
28. C. Wesley and J. Wesley, *Poetical Works*, III:236.

FOR FURTHER CONSIDERATION:

1. What options do we have when there is a controversy in the church, and Scriptures can be credibly cited to support either side of the argument?

2. Why did this controversy end in schism? *Could* separation have been avoided? *Should* it have been avoided?

3. What is the proper relationship between saving faith and good works? Can you explain it to others? How about works of piety? Works of mercy? Means of grace?

4. What are the dangers of putting too much emphasis upon doing good works? What are the dangers of not stressing good works often enough?

5. Clearly, there are times when "waiting upon the Lord" is the proper thing to do—how might we reliably know when that time is?

CHAPTER 12

"God's Everlasting Love"

Controversy over Predestination and Christian Comfort

AT THE SAME TIME the young Methodist movement was riven by controversy over "Stillness" in London, a second controversy erupted in Bristol over the Calvinistic doctrines of the election and predestination. The storm center was the Wesleys' Kingswood School, near Bristol, where a closet Calvinist, John Cennick (1718–55), had recently been made headmaster. Once again, the dispute over theology was made all the more painful because it created distance between the Wesley brothers and some of their oldest and dearest friends, including George Whitefield (1714–70), Selina Hastings, the Countess of Huntingdon, the Welsh evangelist Howell Harris (1714–73), John Cennick, and many others.

Phillip Dawe, *John Cennick* (1785), Mezzotint Print, in the National Library of Wales, from Wikimedia (public domain).

George Whitefield had been one of the original Oxford Methodists. As a college student he began meeting with Charles Wesley for spiritual support and encouragement amidst the young man's difficulties of practicing Christian faith at the university. The university's many temptations, as well as the stiff ridicule Whitefield received for trying to live a pious life, were wearing him down. Charles loaned Whitefield a book that brought about his conversion, and integrated him into the small group that was forming around the Wesleys. Whitefield recalled: "though I had fasted, watched, and

prayed, and received the sacrament so long, yet I never knew what true religion was, till God sent me that excellent treatise by the hands of my never-to-be-forgotten friend."[1] John Wesley Whitefield treated with unusual deference, but Charles he looked upon warmly as his "spiritual father."[2] Upon his graduation George White-field took holy orders in the Church of England and intended to accompany the Wesley brothers to Georgia.[3] When his mission was delayed, George began preaching in various locations in London, with astounding effects. Soon his theatrical and enthusiastic style of preaching drew crowds larger than churches could hold, so Whitefield preached in the fields and city greens. In the spring of 1739, he convinced the Wesley brothers to join him in that new *alfresco* approach. The three men worked in close as-

Joseph Badger, *George Whitefield* (ca. 1745), oil on canvas, at the Harvard University Portrait Gallery, from Wikimedia (public domain).

sociation with each other. They were like "a threefold cord that is not easily broken" (Eccl 4:12) Charles Wesley said.[4]

A torturous path of disagreement and conflict developed between the Wesleys, John Cennick, and Whitefield over the next several years. The dispute between the Wesleys and Whitefield was exacerbated by the fact that Whitefield sailed to America on August 14, 1739 for an evangelistic tour and did not return to England until March 1741. The geographic distance between them provided plenty of room for misunderstanding, hearsay, and gossip to color their communications. It also seems likely that the changing character of their relationship impeded rather than improved the situation; by 1739, a major role reversal had occurred in their three-way relationship. George Whitefield's astounding popularity and success as an evangelist eclipsed that of both his "father in the faith" (Charles Wesley) and his teacher-leader-mentor from the Oxford holy club (John Wesley), and some adjustments are difficult to make. Their subsequent "poaching" of followers from each other's camps caused further resentment and created a few

1. Whitefield, *George Whitefield's Journals*, 46–47.
2. Gillies, *Memoirs of Rev. George Whitefield*, 16.
3. Gillies, *Memoirs of Rev. George Whitefield*, 13–24.
4. C. Wesley, *Letters*, 268.

ugly public scenes. Less public, but also significant, was the fact that White-field and John Wesley tacitly vied for leadership in the fledgling Methodist movement.

There is no mention of Whitefield's Calvinistic understanding of salvation during the Oxford years he shared with the Wesleys; but his emphasis upon God's "sovereign" (and irresistible) grace began to emerge in his subsequent preaching. During his first preaching tour of North America, George Whitefield worked in close cooperation with staunch Calvinists like Jonathon Edwards (a Congregationalist) and William Tenet (a Presbyterian). His association with them confirmed and deepened his own commitment to Calvinism. Three times over the course of a few months, Whitefield wrote to Wesley describing his growing convictions about the controversial doctrines.[5] On March 26, 1740, for example, Whitefield reported to John Wesley: "The doctrine of election, and the final perseverance of those that are truly in Christ, I am ten thousand times more convinced of, if possible, than when I saw you last—You think otherwise: why then should we dispute, when there is no probability of convincing? . . . How many would rejoice, should I join and make a party against you?"[6]

The Wesleys were Arminian champions of God's "free grace" offered to all people, by the prevenient work of God the Holy Spirit. God offered salvation to all people by grace but it could, nonetheless, be refused. The Calvinist and Wesleyan-Arminian soteriologies can both be asserted with the support of Bible passages. Whitefield's "sovereign grace" is most prevalent in the Pauline corpus (notably Rom 8:29–30; 9; Eph 1:13–14), while the Wesleys' "free grace" abounds in the preaching of Jesus in the Gospels (the "whosoevers," John 3:36, etc.) and the General Epistles (Heb 6:1–6; 1 John 1–2). While it is not entirely clear where George Whitefield "got" his Calvinism, the Wesleys' views came straight from the practical theologian of their family, their mother, Susanna Annesley Wesley. In a letter to John Wesley, when he was a young theological student at Oxford, Susanna spelled out her own views on the matter with clarity and precision:

> The doctrine of predestination, as maintained by the rigid Calvinists, is very shocking, and ought utterly to be abhorred; because it directly charges the most Holy God with being the author of sin. . . . For 'tis certainly inconsistent with the justice and goodness of God to lay any man under either a physical or moral necessity of committing sin, and then punish him for

5. Houghton, *George Whitefield's Letters*, 180; Baker, *Works*, 20:11, "From the Rev. George Whitefield," March 26, 1740.

6. Houghton, *George Whitefield's Letters*, March 26, 1740, 155–56.

doing it. "Far be this from thee, O Lord. . . . Shall not the Judge
of all the earth do right?"[7]

Susanna's letter went on to point out that it was the Christian's *approach*
to salvation which had been "predestined" since it was God's plan to save
all people and to "conform them to the image of his Son" (Rom 8). In this
sense, "predestination" did not determine the eternal destiny of particular
individuals. Salvation was based upon the condition that those who would
be saved must respond to the inward call of God's Holy Spirit, in faith and
repentance. "This is the sum of what I believe concerning predestination,"
she wrote, "which I think is agreeable to the analogy of faith [the message
of the Bible], since it never derogates from God's free grace; nor impairs the
liberty of man."[8] Susanna's sons took the very same approach to the controverted topic.

While John was preaching at Newgate on April 26, 1739, from the text
"He that believeth hath everlasting life [John 3:36]," he recalled:

> I was sensibly led, without any previous design, to declare
> strongly and explicitly that God "willeth all men to be *thus*
> saved" and to pray that if these were not the truth of God, he
> would not suffer [allow] the blind to go out of the way; but if it
> were, he would bear witness to his Word. Immediately, one and
> another and another sunk to the earth; they dropped on every
> side as thunderstruck.[9]

So many people were visibly affected by Wesley's message and were relieved
of spiritual burdens of guilt and shame that John felt compelled to return to
the topic of God's universal acceptance once again two days later: "I declared
the free grace of God to about four thousand people, from those words, 'He
that spared not his own Son, but delivered him up for us all, how shall he not
with him also freely give us all things' [Rom 8:32]."[10] John was consistently
preaching *in favor* of the tenet of the universal (as opposed to the limited)
atonement of Christ, and the all-inclusive gospel of God's free grace.

John Wesley's April letter to James Hutton also made it clear what
he was preaching *against*: "On Sunday morning," John wrote, "being so
directed again by lot, I declared openly for the first h[our] *against* 'the horrible decree,' before about four thousand people at the Bowling Green."[11]

---

7. Baker, *Works*, 20:179.

8. Baker, *Works*, 20:180.

9. J. Wesley, *Journal and Diaries*, II:51. Emphasis original.

10. J. Wesley, *Journal and Diaries*, II:56.

11. Baker, *Works*, 20:640. Emphasis added.

The "horrible decree" refers to the Calvinistic notion that just as God had selected particular individuals to enteral salvation so also were others selected for eternal damnation; a "double predestination," so to speak. The sermon John Wesley preached that day was "Free Grace," and it kicked off ripples of controversy and conflict that continued for nearly forty years.

The situation of John Wesley's preaching "Free Grace" was complicated by the fact that it bought him into direct conflict with George Whitfield and was a violation of their agreement not to preach on the topic of predestination for fear of dividing the Methodist movement. But the inner urging John received to preach God "willeth all men to be saved," which Wesley took to be the leading of the Holy Spirit, was very strong. On April 25, 1739, John wrote on "Free Grace." The next day, when he "appealed to God" in prayer about what to do with it, Wesley received no clear answer, so he resorted to casting lots: "The answer was, 'Preach *and* print.' Let Him [God] see to the event."[12]

John Wesley's antipathy toward predestination was based in two main concerns. He believed the Calvinist formulation of the doctrine puts God and Jesus Christ in a horribly wrong light, and that it utterly distorts the nature of Christian life. John was adamant: "On this I join issue with every assenter of it [predestination]. You represent God as worse than the devil—more false, more cruel, more unjust. . . ." Equally alarming to him was the way predestination made Jesus Christ into a liar, and a hypocrite: "For it cannot be denied that He [Christ] everywhere speaks as if He *was willing* that all men should be saved. Therefore, to say He was *not* willing that all men should be saved is to represent him as a mere hypocrite and dissembler."[13] Three times in the same sermon, John Wesley described predestination as "blasphemy" because it makes God seem unjust and depicts Jesus Christ as a liar who promises salvation to all people while He intentionally withholds it from the "non-elect."[14]

John Wesley also believed that the predestinarian approach to salvation completely distorts the nature of Christian life: "this doctrine not only tends to destroy Christian holiness, happiness, and good works, but hath also a direct and manifest tendency to overthrow the whole Christian revelation."[15] These practical concerns were the basis of the Wesleys' utter revulsion toward the doctrine of predestination; it erupted most often when they saw a person using their unconditional election by God as license to do

---

12. Baker, *Works,* 20:640. Emphasis original.

13. J. Wesley, "Free Grace," in *Sermons,* III:556. Emphasis added.

14. J. Wesley, *Sermons,* III:554, 555, 556.

15. J. Wesley, *Sermons,* III: 551–52.

whatever they wanted—even evil—because they believed that nothing they could do or say would vitiate their salvation. A second practical concern was the hopelessness that the Wesleys saw among the poor, outcasts, and beaten-down people for whom it was all too easy to believe they were not among God's elect. In that context, John observed, the doctrine of unconditional election "tends to destroy the comfort of religion, the happiness of Christianity. This is evident as to all those who believe themselves to be reprobated, or who only suspect or fear it."[16]

John Wesley's pamphlet *Free Grace* concluded with a thirty-six-verse poetical polemic by his brother Charles (one of his many) entitled "Universal Redemption." Echoing the same sentiments raised by John, Charles Wesley's attack focused more upon the elitism he saw as being inherent in a gospel that intentionally excluded many of God's good people. In a letter to George Whitefield, John Cennick confirmed both Charles's point of contention as well as the tenacity with which Charles pressed it: "With Universal Redemption, brother Charles pleases the world. Brother John follows him in everything."[17] In Charles's view, the predestinarian soteriology misrepresented the dimensions of Christ's saving death as well as the restorative, liberating power of God's prevenient, free grace:

> For every man he [Christ] tasted death,
> He suffered once for all,
> He calls as many souls as breathe,
> And all may hear the call.
>
> A power to choose, a will to obey,
> Freely his grace restores;
> We may all find the Living Way,
> And call the Savior ours. . . .[18]

In essence, the Wesleys saw the predestinarian soteriology as turning the "good news" of the gospel into "bad news" for many of God's people, and they were not going to stand for it.

Soon George Whitefield received a report, probably from John Cennick, that John Wesley had broken their truce on the topic of predestination: "I hear, honored sir," Whitefield wrote to Wesley, "you are about to print a sermon against predestination. It shocks me to think of it. What will be the consequence but controversy? If people ask me my opinion, what shall I do?

---

16. J. Wesley, *Sermons*, III:549.

17. J. Wesley, *Works* (1872), I:300.

18. J. Wesley, *Sermons*, III:560. Verses 8–9 of 36. This hymn was subsequently republished in the Wesleys' *Hymns and Sacred Poems* of 1740.

I have a critical part to act. God enable me to behave aright. Silence on both sides will be best. It is noised abroad already that there is a division between you and me. Oh! My heart within me is grieved!"[19] John had already printed the first pamphlet edition of his sermon *Free Grace* but he acquiesced to Whitefield's request for silence and did not print a second edition until a year later when the controversy heated up once gain.

Why did John Wesley decide to "preach and publish" against predestination in April 1739, when he knew it would likely cause a major public controversy? Here, I think, we see the "enthusiast" side of "the reasonable enthusiast" at work. His revulsion at the Calvinistic gospel was as deep and genuine as was his anger at the harm he saw it causing people who lived hopeless and precarious lives. On that basis, it was relatively easy for John to follow what he took to be the leading of the Holy Spirit to "preach and publish." Other less obvious issues were also involved; in attacking the Wesleys' Arminian soteriology, Whitefield and the Calvinists were attacking what their mother, Susanna Wesley, had taught them. It's very likely, at some subconscious level, it felt like an attack upon their saintly mother.

During late 1740 and early 1741 it must have seemed like the Methodist movement was going to implode. While the predestination controversy simmered in Bristol, John Wesley hurried back to London to try to quell the Stillness Controversy. As Calvinism swept through the Methodist Societies, Charles tried to hold the Bristol and nearby Kingswood Societies together and to win over as many people as he could to the Wesleyan version of "Free Grace." Charles mounted a homiletical and hymnological assault against the Calvinistic doctrines of predestination, election, and eternal security while John Cennick, Howel Harris, and others preached and taught in support of them.

On December 3, 1740, Charles confided to his journal: "Things are come to a crisis at Kingswood. . . . They tell me plainly they will separate from me if I preach one word against final perseverance or hint at the possibility of a justified person's falling from grace."[20] A week later, Charles reported: "I wrote my brother a full account of the predestinarian party, their practices and designs, particularly 'to have a church within themselves, and to give themselves the sacrament in bread and water.'"[21] On February 24, 1741, John Wesley met with the Kingswood Methodist Society and expelled forty-two "disorderly walkers" from it. The final "show down" came on March 7,

19. Baker, "From the Revd George Whitefield, London, June 25, 1739," in *Works*, 20:662.

20. Baker, *Works*, 20:662.

21. Baker, *Works*, 20:293.

when, after a rancorous session of charges and countercharges, members of the Kingswood Society were asked to decide whether they wanted to be a part of a Calvinistic or a Wesleyan-Arminian Society. After a brief period of prayer, John Cennick and fifty-two others voted with their feet by walking out of the Kingswood Society—never to return.[22]

While George Whitefield was preaching in America, two strongly worded anonymous treatises against the Wesleys and their Arminian theology appeared. The first, *'Free Grace' Indeed!* (May 1740) was a direct assault upon Wesley's *Free Grace* sermon. It also contained personal affronts and innuendos assailing John Wesley's motives and character. It was almost certainly penned by an angry Whitefield, for immediate circulation in America, and the tone of this letter added more heat to the controversy.[23] The second treatise, *A Letter to the Rev. Mr. John Westly, Occasioned by His Sermon against Predestination*, was written by "Christianus," on Christmas Eve 1740. It circulated in America and then was republished in London in May 1741. The *Letter to the Rev. Mr. John Wesley* was easily traced directly to George Whitefield, and it too contained as much personal attack as theological argumentation.[24] When George Whitefield arrived in England, March 11, 1741, he almost immediately followed through on his promise to preach and publish against his former mentors. When he saw the result of the Wesleys' campaign against Calvinism, which was carried out in his absence, Whitefield began a spirited counteroffensive: "Many, very many of my spiritual children," he complained to Howell Harris, "are prejudiced by the dear Messrs Wesleys' dressing up the doctrine of election in such horrible colors that they will neither hear, see, nor give me the least assistance."[25]

Whitefield's attempt to win back his "spiritual children" began the day after he arrived in England, when he was offered a courtesy call in Charles Wesley's pulpit. George used the opportunity to preach three anti-Wesleyan doctrines: "predestination, perseverance, and the necessity of sinning" while Charles Wesley sat beside him in utter incredulity. "Afterwards," Charles reported, "I *mildly* expostulated with him, asking if he would commend me for preaching the opposite doctrine in his Orphan House, protesting again the publishing his answer to you, and laboring for peace to the utmost of my power. [I] asked whether he held reprobation, which he avowed, as also his intention of preaching it upon the housetop."[26] The "mildly" part

22. J. Wesley, *Journal and Diaries*, II:186–87.

23. Maddock, "Solving a Transatlantic Puzzle?," 1–15.

24. Harrington, "Friendship under Fire," 167–81.

25. Whitefield, *Works*, I:256–57.

26. Whitefield, *Works*, I:256–57. Emphasis added.

of Charles's report is harder to believe than the " I . . . expostulated" aspect. Three months later, Charles Wesley received similar rough treatment from his Calvinistic friend, Howell Harris, who contradicted the Wesleys' Arminian doctrine from Charles' own pulpit, in front of him.[27] Charles brought Harris's sermon to a sudden conclusion by starting up a rousing Wesleyan hymn; while the congregation sang, Wesley watched as one of the ushers helped Mr. Harris find the door. Afterwards, Charles "acknowledged the grace given to our dear brother Harris and excused his estrangement from me through the wickedness of his counselors." But Charles never offered Harris his pulpit again, and privately told him: "to be plain, *I will sooner die* than consent to your preaching false doctrine to my flock."[28]

Whitefield's *A Letter to the Rev. Mr. John Wesley* depicted Wesley as foolish and superstitious for relying upon casting lots to make important decisions. He also impugned Wesley's character since John had agreed to remain silent about his antipathy for predestination and then subsequently did not.[29] Whitefield's published reply to Wesley sounded so much like a personal affront that an irritated Susanna Wesley penned and published *Some Remarks on a Letter from the Rev. Mr. Whitefield to the Rev. Mr. Wesley in a Letter from a Gentlewoman to Her Friend* (1741) in defense of her sons and the Methodist movement.[30]

In view of Charles Wesley's strenuous campaign against Calvinism in Bristol Methodism and his publication of two series of anti-Calvinistic hymns, it is no wonder that Whitefield lamented: "Dear brother Charles is *more and more rash.* He has lately printed some very bad hymns."[31] The heated confrontations Charles Wesley had with the Calvinists contributed to his growing "more and more rash," but so also did the failings he saw among them. The first of these was their "narrowness of spirit"; it was a spiritual elitism that said, in effect, "I'm saved—and you're not" and gave a person a sense of spiritual superiority. Closely related to their elitism was the lack of love Charles claimed to see in the predestination party; "the poison of Calvin has drunk up their spirit of love," he charged.[32]

The "very bad hymns" George Whitefield complained about were Charles Wesley's two separate volumes of *Hymns on God's Everlasting Love* (1741, 1742). The implication of Charles's title, as well as many of his

---

27. C. Wesley, *Manuscript Journal*, I:316.

28. C. Wesley, *Manuscript Journal*, I:317. Emphasis original.

29. Whitefield, *Letter to the Rev. Mr. John* Wesley, 12.

30. S. Wesley, *Complete Writings*, 464–84.

31. Houghton, *George Whitefield's Letters*, 510. Emphasis added.

32. C. Wesley, *Manuscript Journal*, I:292;

hymns, was simply that the Wesleys preached a God of everlasting love and acceptance, while Whitefield and the Calvinists preached a God of wrath and exclusion. The little word "all" reverberates throughout these hymns, as Charles Wesley used it to demolish the popular appeal of Calvinism by contrasting it with the "all"-inclusive gospel of God's love and grace. The first hymn of the collection exemplified the rest:

> Father, whose *Everlasting Love*
> Thy only Son for sinners gave,
>   Whose grace to *all* did *freely* move,
> And sent Him down *a world* to save.
>   Help us Thy mercy to extol,
> Immense, unfathom'd unconfined;
>   To praise the Lamb who died for *all*
> The *general Savior of all mankind.* . . .
>   Jesus hath said, we *all* shall hope,
> Preventing grace for all is free;
>   "And I, if I be lifted up,
> I will *draw all men* unto me."[33]

Hymnologist John Rattenbury credited Charles Wesley's hymns with discrediting popular Calvinism in England: "they made it incredible to reason, and repulsive to the heart of decent people," he wrote.[34]

Controversy between the Whitefieldite Calvinistic Methodists and Wesleyan Arminians ebbed and flowed throughout the next three decades. Thankfully there also were periods of sweet reunion and fellowship between the Wesleys and Whitefield. In November 1755, for example, John wrote: "Mr. Whitefield called upon me. Disputings are now no more. We love one another and join hand in and to promote the cause of our common Master."[35] But the embers of controversy flamed up again and again, due in part to the fact that, as Gerorge Whitefield observed, "Busybodies, on both sides, blew up the coals."[36] Additional waves of controversy erupted in the 1760s, and again in the 1770s, as a misunderstanding about good works and salvation ("the Minutes Controversy") further divided the Methodist movement.

In one last grand gesture of magnanimity, George Whitefield, in his will, stipulated that John Wesley should preach his funeral sermon, in his own London Tabernacle. Whitefield's death on September 30, 1770 (in

---

33. C. Wesley and J. Wesley, *Poetical Works*, III:3. Emphasis original.

34. Rattenbury, *Evangelical Doctrines*, 100–101.

35. J. Wesley, *Journal and Diaries*, IV:33.

36. Tyerman, *Life of Rev. George Whitefield*, I:475.

Newburyport, Massachusetts), was strategically ill-timed since it occurred in the midst of still another controversy between the Wesleyans and White-fieldites. The Calvinistic Methodists had already begun circling their wag-ons against him when John Wesley stood up to preach Whitefield's funeral sermon on November 17, 1770. Wesley tried to keep to the ecumenical tone of Whitefield's invitation by pressing for unity and reconciliation. After a long and glowing eulogy, John Wesley urged: "let us keep close to the grand scriptural doctrines which he [Whitefield] everywhere delivered."[37] Wesley acknowledged: "there are many doctrines of a less essential nature, with regard to which even the sincere children of God . . . are and have been divided for many ages. In these we may think and let think." John even quoted Whitefield himself to the effect they should "agree to disagree" about the more controverted Christian beliefs. He urged: "[L]et us hold fast the essentials of 'the faith which was once delivered to the saints,' and which this champion of God [George Whitefield] so strongly insisted on at all times and in all places."[38]

But instead of sounding like a peace offering, the Whitefieldites heard John Wesley's message as still another salvo in the war of words. Contro-versy erupted again as the Whitefieldites, like William Romaine, attacked the Wesleyans and their theology through his *The Gospel Magazine*. In reply, John Wesley began an informational campaign, as he penned and published *The Question: "What Is an Arminian?" Answered by a Lover of Free Grace, in London* (1770). A weary sounding John Wesley wrote with the voice of experience: "To say, 'this man is an Arminian,' has the same effect on many hearers, as to say, 'this is a mad dog.' It puts them into a fright at once: they run away from him with all speed and diligence: and will hardly stop, unless it be to throw a stone at the dreadful, mischievous animal."[39] When John de-scribed "the undeniable difference" between Calvinists and Arminians, he pointed to unconditional election, by which God chose people for salvation and damnation, and the Arminian "conditional predestination."[40] Wesley observed, "the three questions [separating them] come into one, 'is predes-tination absolute or conditional?' The Arminians believe, it is conditional; the Calvinists, that it is absolute."[41] John Wesley's treatise closed with still another appeal for peace—which did not materialize.

37. J. Wesley, *Sermons*, III:341.
38. J. Wesley, *Sermons*, II:341.
39. J. Wesley, *Works* (1872), X:358.
40. J. Wesley *Works* (1872), X:359.
41. J. Wesley, *Works* (1872), X:360.

The Calvinistic Controversy caused deep divisions and alienation between the Wesleys and several of their closest friends. The war of words harmed the movement—from both within and without. It created anger, pride, distrust, and division that sapped the energy of the movement, and raised serious questions about the credibility of Methodism in the eyes of their eighteenth-century contemporaries. On the positive side of the ledger, the controversy forced the Methodists to think through their approach to salvation and to articulate it more carefully. The distinction between "irresistible" and "prevenient grace" was hammered out on the anvil of heated conversations where each opposite party ardently affirmed that God's grace is "free."

The controversy demonstrated the connection between one's understanding of salvation, their mental picture of God, and the way a person lives out her/his Christian life. While it was possible to stack up Bible texts and productive results on both sides of the argument, it was the elitism and exclusion that the Wesleys heard and saw in the Calvinistic message that caused them to fight so hard against it. They also had a visceral revulsion to a gospel they saw as horribly misrepresenting the God, as well as the Savior, whom they loved and followed. They saw themselves as rejecting a message that so easily turned God's grace into a blank check for bad behavior (once you are saved you are always saved). Equally distressing was a loveless pride that valued being "right" more than being righteous and loving. But the Wesley brothers also failed to live up to their own standards of the "catholic spirit" or Christian love at many points of the controversy, and there was/is a lesson for us in that aspect as well.

FOR FURTHER CONSIDERATION:

1. Do you see much difference between stressing God's sovereign grace, which cannot be refused, and prevenient grace, which can? What are the implications?

2. This controversy could not be resolved by simply consulting the Scriptures. What other implications entered in? How do "implications" affect your own thought processes?

3. Personal elements contributed to the inability to "agree to disagree" in this controversy. Do you see these elements in contentions or decisions? When and how can they be avoided?

4. After thirty years of contention, John Wesley was willing to suggest predestination was a doctrine not worth fighting or dividing over, but

others reached the opposite conclusion. How can controversy shape people's views in such opposite ways?

5. Are there some Christian beliefs and practices that are not worth arguing about or dividing over? What are they? How did you decide what these are?

CHAPTER 13

"They Made Perfection Stink"

Controversy over the Meaning of Christian Perfection

As an elderly John Wesley recounted the history of the Methodist movement, his thoughts went back to its beginnings in the Oxford Holy Club: "in
1729 two young men [John and Charles Wesley], reading the Bible, saw they
could not be saved without holiness, followed after it, and incited others so
to do."[1] Six months prior to the end his life, John Wesley wrote, "I am glad
brother D—has more light with regard to full sanctification. This doctrine is
the *Grand Depostum*, which God has lodged with the people called Methodists and for the sake of propagating this doctrine he appeared to have raised
us up."[2] These two statements were like bookends to the Wesleys' long and
active pursuit of "holiness of heart and mind." Sanctification, holiness, or
Christian perfection was the reason those "two young men" began their
long walk with God and when they "incited others so do" the Methodist
movement was born. Sanctification, or "scriptural holiness," was also central
to the mission statement the Methodists hammered out at their first Annual
Conference where they agreed "not to form any new sect; but to reform the
nation, particularly the Church, and *to spread scriptural holiness over the
land*."[3]

"Bible bigots,"[4] as they were described in derision at Oxford, the Wesleys insisted upon using the controverted and often misunderstood Bible

1. J. Wesley, *Works* (1872), VIII:299.

2. J. Wesley, *Letters*, VIII:238.

3. J. Wesley, *Works* (1872), VIII:299. Emphasis original.

4. J. Wesley, *Works* (1872), VIII:299.

word "perfection" to name their core concept, even though it often confused more often than it clarified. The term, and the mission it gave them, came straight from the mouth of Jesus: "Be ye therefore perfect, even as your Father which is in heaven is perfect" (Matt 5:48); so they clung to it tenaciously. A large part of the problem was the fact that few others were/ are the talented linguists that John and Charles Wesley were. They knew that the "perfection" (*telieios*) in the New Testament Greek could, and perhaps should, be translated as "whole, complete, or mature." This "perfection," they ascertained, was a synonym for the *agape* or "selfless love" epitomized by the powerful words of 1 Corinthians 13:

> Love is patient; love is kind; love is not envious or boastful or arrogant or rude. It does not insist on its own way; it is not irritable or resentful; it does not rejoice in wrongdoing, but rejoices in the truth. It bears all things, believes all things, hopes all things, endures all things. Love never ends. . . . And now faith, hope, and love abide, these three; and the greatest of these is love.[5]

The Johannine literature of the New Testament taught the Wesleys about the interconnection between God's love *(agapé)* and perfection *(telieios)*. "God is love; and he that dwelleth in love dwelleth in God, and God in him" (1 John 4:15–16), hence "whosoever keepeth His word, in him verily is the love of God perfected" (1 John 2:5); therefore: "If we love one another, God dwelleth in us, and his love is perfected in us" (1 John 4:12). Because this "perfection" is in and by God's love, Christian perfection most often described a process instead of a static state, so phraseology like "perfec*ting* love" is probably more helpful. Several other terms like "holiness," "sanctification," "perfection in love," or "perfect love," were viewed as theological synonyms.[6]

When it came time to describe the effects of this "perfection," the early Methodists often pointed to the "greatest commandment" (Matt 22:26–40). Their synthesis of New Testament terms and concepts was reflected in the definition of Christian perfection developed by the Methodist Annual Conference of 1759:

Question: "What is Christian Perfection?"

Answer: "The loving God with all our heart, mind, and strength.

This implies that no wrong temper [attitude], none contrary to

---

5. 1 Cor 13:4–13 (NRSV).

6. Tyson, *Charles Wesley on Sanctification*, 157–79.

love, remains in the soul; and that all the thoughts, words, and actions, are governed by pure love."[7]

The multiplicity of expressions the early Methodists used to name and describe their cardinal concept and guiding vision undoubtedly contributed to the confusion and controversy about it. But this same linguistic variety also signaled the deep spiritual interconnection of concepts like scriptural holiness, sanctification, perfect love, Christian perfection, and so on. The Wesleys found it was sometimes much easier for the Methodists to define Christian perfection by saying what it was *not*: "Christian Perfection . . . does not imply (as some men seem to have imagined) an exemption either from ignorance, or mistake, or infirmities or temptations. Indeed, it is only another term for holiness. They are two names for the same thing."[8]

The Wesleys' proclamation of Christian perfection drew heavy criticism from Calvinistic contemporaries like George Whitefield,[9] for whom original sin was such a determinative theological constant that a person's actual righteousness through their growth in God's grace was a controverted concept. Their sin-centered approach to theology carried with it a fundamentally negative view of humans and human nature. But a closer look at the creation narratives of the Hebrew Scriptures suggested (to the Wesleys) something different; humans were "created in the image of God" (Lat. *imago Dei*, Gen 1:26), and human nature and God-given identity—even when flawed s a result of sin—could and should be celebrated: "I will praise Thee," wrote the Psalmist, "for I am fearfully and wonderfully made; marvelous are Thy works, and that my soul knoweth right well" (Ps 139:14). The writer of the Hebrews Epistle also voiced a God-centered theology of human nature: "Thou madest him a little lower than the angels, Thou crownedst him with glory and honor, and did set him over the works of Thy hands" (Heb 2:7).

Starting from a theological foundation built upon original sin, the Calvinists stressed the depth of human inability apart from God, and how very much people always need God's grace to live well. Because our sinful nature struggles against our God-given identity, all people are "double-minded" (Jas 1:7). They, like St. Paul, "delight in the law of God after the inward man; but I see another law in my members, warring against the law of my mind, and bringing me into captivity to the law of sin which is in my members. O wretched man that I am! who shall deliver me from the body of this

---

7. J. Wesley, *Works* (1872), XI:394.

8. J. Wesley, "Christian Perfection," in *Sermons,* II:104. See also *A Plain Account of Christian Perfection* (1766) in J. Wesley, *Works* (1872), XI:366–448.

9. Houghton, *George Whitefield's Letters,* 212: "What a fond conceit it is to cry down the doctrine of final perseverance and cry up Perfection."

death?" (Rom 7:22–24). Who, indeed? Paul knew: "I thank God through Jesus Christ our Lord. So then with the mind, I myself serve the law of God" (Rom 7:25). In Jesus Christ there is restoration, there is victory over sin.

The Wesleys and the Methodists embraced a God-centered understanding of human nature, and human life in contrast to the sin-centered approach. They learned it from their love of the Bible, especially the preaching of Jesus in the Gospels and in the General Epistles. They found it echoed in early Eastern Christian writers, like Origen, Athanasius, Gregory Nanzianus, Gregory of Nyssa, and John Chrysostom.[10] For the Wesleyans, this meant that "original righteousness" (one's true God-given identity), and not "original sin," was the controlling concept of their soteriology. While they affirmed original sin and the catastrophic effects of the Edenic fall, when it came to human salvation they also believed God's prevenient grace reached out to all people to "woo" them into restored and healing relationship with God in Jesus Christ. But unlike Reformed "sovereign grace," God's prevenient grace can, tragically, be refused. This emphasis gave the Wesleyans a higher and grace-filled estimation of human capacity and ability than tht of their Calvinistic counterparts. Hence, Christian life in the Methodists' view was thought of as being more a call to victorious living, in which sin is overcome through growth and maturation, and less as an ongoing struggle and stalemate against sin and self and the world.

Their theological starting point in "original righteousness" also gave the Wesleyans a different soteriological aim: the Calvinists. If the guilt of sin is the perennial problem of human life then pardon and forgiveness become the main solution through salvation. But if the loss of "original righteousness" or "the image of God" is the main concern then what has been lost must be found, and the goal of salvation becomes inner healing, renewal, and restoration of that original God-given nature. In the Wesleys' view, the "imputed righteousness" of Christ, so aptly stressed by their Calvinist colleagues as change of standing before God (justified, pardon), was also "imparted" to the Christian believer through the healing presence of God the Holy Spirit, which began a new birth and Christlikeness within them.[11] There is, declared John Wesley, "a real as well as a relative change" associated with the believer who comes to faith: "We are inwardly renewed by the power of God. We feel the 'love of God shed abroad in our heart by God the Holy Ghost which is given unto us,' producing love to all mankind. . . . In a word, changing the earthly, sensual, devilish mind into 'the mind which was

---

10. See Campbell, *John Wesley*, 23–73; and Kimbrough, "Charles Wesley," 165–83.

11. See J. Wesley, "The Lord Our Righteousness," in *Sermons*, #20, I:452–63.

in Christ Jesus."[12] The powerfully succinct saying of St. Athanasius summed up the Wesleyan soteriological vision quite well: "[Christ] became what we are, to make us what He is."[13]

In the Wesleyan theological model, being "forgiven" (justified) is just the beginning of salvation but it isn't the end, because humans were created to be "partakers of the divine nature" (2 Pet 2:4) by having the life of Christ formed within. Charles Wesley's hymns are particularly replete with images and metaphors for annunciating God's therapeutic grace that heals and restores human hearts. One of Charles Wesley's most famous hymns, "Love Divine, All Loves Excelling," expressed well this emphasis upon God's restorative love:[14]

> 1. Love divine, all loves excelling,
> Joy of heaven to earth come down,
> Fix in us thy humble dwelling,
> All thy faithful mercies crown;
> Jesu, thou art all compassion,
> Pure unbounded love thou art,
> Visit us with thy salvation,
> Enter every trembling heart.
>
> 2. Breathe, O breathe thy loving Spirit
> Into every troubled breast,
> Let us all in thee inherit,
> Let us find that second rest:
> Take away our power of sinning,
> Alpha and Omega be,
> End of faith as its beginning,
> Set our hearts at liberty.
>
> 3. Come, Almighty to deliver,
> Let us all thy life receive,
> Suddenly return, and never,
> Never more thy temples leave.
> Thee we would be always blessing,
> Serve thee as thy hosts above,
> Pray, and praise thee without ceasing,

12. J. Wesley, "The Scripture way of Salvation," in *Sermons*, #43, II:158.

13. Tyson, *Great Athanasius*, 59–63.

14. C. Wesley, "Hymn IX," in *Hymns for Those That Seek*, 11–12. When John published it in the 1780 MHB, as #374, he omitted the somewhat controversial verse #2, which originally read "Take away our bent of sinning."

Glory in thy perfect love.

4. Finish then thy new creation,
Pure and sinless let us be,

5. Let us see thy great salvation,
Perfectly restor'd in thee;
Chang'd from glory into glory,
Till in heaven we take our place,
Till we cast our crowns before thee,
Lost in wonder, love, and praise![15]

Despite John Wesley's many explanations and attempts at clarification, "Christian perfection" continued to be a point of contention, both in and outside of the Methodist movement. It was a main topic of conversation and deliberation at the first Methodist Annual Conferences in 1744, and again in 1745 and 1746. During the fourth session of the 1746 conference it was still a point of contention because "several persons were present who did not believe the doctrine of perfection, we agreed to examine it from the foundation."[16] Their thorough conversation and debate about the doctrine indicated that there were three main points of contention among the early Methodists about Christian perfection: 1) is it sinless perfection? 2) is it instantaneous or gradual? and 3) does it occur only at death—or can it come at any time? Debate about the doctrine was often carried on at a more rudimentary level: "there is no such thing as perfection in this world."[17]

As the in-house contention among the Methodists about holiness or Christian perfection continued into the early 1760s, two events occurred that made conversation extremely public again. The first of these erupted when two Methodist lay preachers, Thomas Maxfield and George Bell, became increasing radical and unguarded in their preaching about Christian perfection. The second event occurred as Charles Wesley published his *magnum opus*—a two-volume, poetical Bible commentary entitled *Short Hymns on Select Passages of Scripture* (1762).

Maxfield and Bell were charismatic preachers and worship leaders whose proclivities drifted closer and closer toward rank "enthusiasm" in the opening years of the 1760s. Both men developed an air of spiritual superiority about themselves, which gave them a popular following of parishioners and seemed to encourage then to make increasingly extravagant claims

15. C. Wesley, "Hymn IX," in *Hymns for Those That Seek*, 11–12. Cf. https://www.umc.org/en/content/love-divine-all-loves-excelling-by-charles-wesley.

16. J. Wesley, *Works* (1872), XIII:160.

17. J. Wesley, *Works* (1872), XIII:167.

about their own perfection and spiritual powers.[18] In July 1761, John Wesley found himself forced to preach and teach extensively against the conception of sinless perfection, stressing that there is never a time when a Christian does not need "the atoning blood, therefore all men need to say daily, 'Forgive us our trespasses.'"[19]

Roland Houston, *Thomas Maxfield Methodist Preacher* (London, 1772), a mezzotint print after painting by Thomas Beach in the National Portrait Gallery, London, from Wikimedia (public domain).

On December 29, 1761, John met with a few of the most strident advocates for unqualified perfection in London. Thomas Maxfield, who was one of the most ardent preachers of perfection, did not attend that meeting, which roused John's suspicions about an impending schism or blow-up. Charles had been privately warning John of the enthusiasm lurking under the surface in the London Society for more than a year.[20] Charles was concerned because when John Walsh and Rev. John Berridge met with George Bell on January 12, 1762, Bell told them: "God had given him the gift of healing which he had already practiced and of raising from the dead, which he should perform in God's time. That the millennium was begun and he should never die."[21] On February 17, 1762, a member of West Street Chapel Band testified that he had been made perfect when George Bell had prayed and laid holy hands upon him, and the next week John Walsh testified to the same thing. Seemingly unperturbed, John Wesley examined Walsh and renewed his class membership ticket as a card-carrying Methodist in good standing.[22]

Meanwhile, Charles Wesley continued to work in Bristol, where he was putting the finishing touches on his *Short Hymns on Select Passages of Scripture*. The "Advertisement" or preface indicated Charles was aware of the growing "enthusiasm" of the London Perfectionists, and intended to enter the lists against them: "Several of the hymns [in that collection] are

18. Lloyd, "Cloud of Perfect Witnesses," 117–36.
19. Lloyd, "Cloud of Perfect Witnesses," 136–37.
20. Lloyd, "Cloud of Perfect Witnesses," 124.
21. Lloyd, "Cloud of Perfect Witnesses," 124.
22. Lloyd, "Cloud of Perfect Witnesses," 125.

intended to prove, and several to guard, the doctrine of Christian Perfection," he wrote, "I durst not publish one without the other."[23] Charles intended to "guard, the doctrine of Christian Perfection" from enthusiasm, and admitted: "I use some severity; not against particular persons, but against Enthusiasts and Antinomians, who, by not living up to their profession [of faith], give abundant occasion to them that seek it, and cause the truth to be evil spoken of."[24]

Charles's *Short Hymns* was his first public statement on the doctrine of Christian perfection since the debates of the 1740s. Although his brother John repeatedly claimed he and Charles had identical views on perfection, it was clear from the *Short Hymns* that this was not entirely true. Charles's position was exactly opposite John's on each of the three controverted issues debated at the 1746 Annual Conference: 1) Christian perfection and "the article of death"; 2) "sinless perfection"—based on John Wesley's definition of outward sin as "a voluntary transgression of a known law of God"[25]; and 3) whether Christian perfection was an instantaneous event that came upon a person by faith.[26] Charles had come to believe perfection was most typically a gradual life process that became complete when the human body is laid down in triumphant and faith-filled death. Nor is there any indication that Charles embraced his brother's carefully nuanced volitional definition of sin that allowed John to consider the possibility of a certain kind of sinlessness in this life.[27] More representative of Charles's mature view was his "Short Hymn" on Matthew 13:33, which likened Christian perfection to the gospel leaven, which gradually spreads divine life throughout the Christian's heart and life:

> That heavenly principle within,
> > Doth it at once its power exert,
> At once root out the seed of sin,
> > And spread perfection through the heart?
> No; but a gradual life it sends,
> > Diffusive through the faithful soul,
> To actions, words, and thoughts extends,
> > And slowly sanctifies the whole.[28]

23. C. Wesley and J. Wesley, *Poetical Works*, IX:vii.

24. C. Wesley and J. Wesley, *Poetical Works*, IX:viii.

25. J. Wesley, "The Great Privilege" in *Sermons*, #19, part II, 2, I:436.

26. J. Wesley, *Works* (1872), XIII:167.

27. Tyson, *Charles Wesley on Sanctification*, 227–301.

28. C. Wesley and J. Wesley, *Poetical Works*, IX:275.

No wonder that John Wesley wrote to his disciple, Dorothy Furly, to warn her: "Take care you are not hurt by anything in the *Short Hymns* contrary to the doctrines you have already long received."[29] Charles's 1762 "Advertisement" also intimated about his failing health: "God having graciously laid His hand upon my body, and disabled me for the principal work of ministry [his incessant itinerancy], has thereby given me an unexpected occasion of writing the following hymns."[30] His own ongoing battle with ill health prompted Charles to add the issue of suffering to the Wesleyan conversation about Christian perfection.[31]

By August 1762, Charles had arrived in London and was trying to rein in the extremists in John's absence. Then, in October, John wrote to Thomas Maxfield and the others more forcefully than he had responded to them in person by enumerating what he liked and what he disliked about their doctrine and behavior. "I like your doctrine of Perfection, or pure love—love excluding all sin. Your insisting that it is merely by *faith*; that consequently it is *instantaneous* (though preceded and followed by a gradual work), and that it may be now, at this instant,"[32] he wrote. John also had nine criticisms for Thomas Maxfield and his associates, many of which had to do with their perceived arrogance, pride, and fomenting division among the London Methodists. But other matters were overshadowed by their rank enthusiasm. John exclaimed, "I dislike your supposing man may be as perfect 'as an angel,' that he can be *absolutely* perfect; that he can be *infallible*, or above being tempted; or that the moment he is pure in heart he *cannot fall* from it."[33]

John made several subsequent attempts to curtail the claims of the enthusiasts and to reconcile them with the London Methodist Society, but to no avail. When George Bell proclaimed that the end of the world would occur on February 28, 1763, it made the London papers. John Wesley wrote open letters to the editor of the *London Chronicle* on January 7 and February 9, 1763, publicly denouncing Maxfield and Bell and trying to distance them from the Methodist movement. He was trying to save the Methodists' (and his own) tarnished reputations.[34] John's terse journal entry for February 21, 1763 indicates a formal separation had already occurred: "The three next days I spent in the tedious work of transcribing the names of the society," he wrote. "I found about thirty of those who thought they were saved from sin

---

29. J. Wesley, *Letters*, IV:189.
30. C. Wesley and J. Wesley, *Poetical Works*, IX:vii.
31. Cruickshank, *Pain, Passion and Faith*.
32. J. Wesley, *Journal and Diaries*, IV:394.
33. J. Wesley, *Journal and Diaries*, IV:394. Emphasis original.
34. J. Wesley, *Letters*, IV:200–203.

had separated from the brethren. But above four hundred who witnessed the same confession seemed more united than ever."[35]

The fallout from the controversy, however, was incalculable. Despite John Wesley's disclaimers, it spread from London throughout the Methodist movement to simmer in other cities as well. Confusion about Christian perfection continued throughout the entire Methodist movement. Because clear consensus and unity on the topic was never achieved, many pious people were spiritually harmed by false teaching or the controversy related to it. Others were utterly disillusioned by John Wesley's mishandling of the situation. Soon the Wesleys and their supporters were embarrassed into silence and inactivity by the controversy. A full four years after the London schism, John Wesley still lamented to Thomas Rankin by letter: "I know not when we shall see an end of the advantage which Satan gained by their [Bell and Maxfield] means. They made the very name of Perfection stink in the nostrils even of those who loved and honored it before."[36]

Over time, the difficult terminology and complicated nature of preaching Christian perfection caused subsequent generations of Methodists to soften the sharp edges of the doctrine, and they became more apt to preach progressive perfection using terminology and metaphors based in maturation and restorative health. This attempt to back away from the more difficult language about Christian perfection *also* caused controversies within the Methodist movement as revival-oriented segments of the movement, like the Primitive Methodists (UK, 1807), the Wesleyan Methodists (1841), Free Methodists (1860), the Church of the Nazarene (1906), the Salvation Army (1865), the Church of God (1886), and Church of God in Christ (1897) each in their own way believed Methodism had jettisoned its cardinal emphasis. Each of those aforementioned groups broke with mainstream Methodism to form new Wesleyan denominations in the pursuit of holiness. This historic controversy about Christian perfection lives on in the questions often asked of clergy preparing to serve in the Wesleyan churches: "Are you going on to perfection? Do you expect to be made perfect in love in this life? Are you earnestly striving after it? Are you resolved to devote yourself wholly to God and his work?[37]

---

35. J. Wesley, *Journal and Diaries*, IV:407.

36. J. Wesley, *Letters*, V:38.

37. United Methodist Church, *Book of Discipline*, para 336.

FOR FURTHER CONSIDERATION:

1. To what degree *do* we need to use "Bible words to describe Bible doctrines?"

2. Is Christian perfection or the "holiness of heart and life" the *grand depositum* of your faith? Do you, do we, make that clear to ourselves and others today?

3. How much basic agreement among ourselves is necessary for us to also be able give each other significant latitude to express and live our faith in a way that seems best to each of us?

4. It is clear that extremism of various sorts has been associated with Christian perfection; what might that look like in our own context?

5. What are the dangers inherent in losing sight of this central, unifying, and divisive belief?

CHAPTER 14

"Whether It Be Lawful or Not"
Controversy over Ecclesiastical Separation and Schism

JOHN AND CHARLES WESLEY were "Church of England men" as people said in those days. Not only were they Anglican priests in good standing, they both had a deep personal love for the church. They imbibed this ardor from their parents, both of whom were raised as Puritans and then converted to Anglicanism as young adults—at great personal cost. Samuel and Susanna Annesley Wesley embraced the Church of England (COE) and her practices with the passion of new converts, and their fervor permeated their home. Charles experienced an extra dose of Anglicanism from his eldest brother, Samuel Jr., who was like a foster father to him during his prep school years. "A strict Churchman," as Charles described him, "who brought me up in his own principles."[1] John Wesley often expressed a similar loyalty: "I declare once more that I live and die a member of the Church of England, and that none who regard my judgment or advice will ever separate from it."[2] "I am a Church-of-England man," he wrote Henry Moore, "and as I said fifty years ago so I say still, in the Church I will live and die, *unless* I am thrust out."[3]

When in 1739 "a serious clergyman" of the COE asked John Wesley wherein the Methodists differed from the church, John gave his stock answer: "To the best of my knowledge, none."[4] Wesley went on to describe the

1. Tyson, *Charles Wesley: A Reader*, 59.

2. Davies, *Works of John Wesley*, 9:540.

3. J. Wesley, *Letters*, VIII:58 (emphasis original); cf., 140; IV:312; VII:163; J. Wesley, *Sermons*, IV:82.

4. J. Wesley, *Journal and Diaries*, II:96.

Methodist mission as one of reviving "inward religion," "the renewal of our heart after the image of Him that created us."[5] The Methodist "Rules" (1743) for their small groups reflected the Wesleys' commitment and connection to the church by insisting on the following for the Methodists: "1) To be at Church and at the Lord's table every week, and at every public meeting of the Bands. 2) To attend the ministry of the word every morning, unless distance, business, or sickness prevent."[6]

But the question of separation from the Church of England dogged early Methodism almost from the outset. It loomed in the background of the "Minutes of Conversation" from their first annual Conference (1744) where the preachers asked themselves, "Do we separate from the Church?" The official answer was, "We conceive not. We hold communion therein for conscience's sake, by constantly attending both the Word preached, and the Sacraments therein."[7] The same "Methodist Minutes" also reflected on public opinion: "What then do they [non-Methodists] mean who say, 'You separate from the Church?'" "We cannot certainly tell" was the reply.[8] This conversation necessarily led to the question of the Methodists' obedience to the Anglican bishops: "How is it our duty to obey the bishops?" Answer: "In all things indifferent. And on this ground of obeying them, we should observe the canons [of church law], so far as we can with a *safe conscience.*"[9] The early Methodists professed loyalty to the COE, but it was a qualified loyalty! Their equivocation became more apparent the next year when the annual conference asked: "What if he [the Bishop] produces a law against your preaching?" Answer: "I am to obey God rather than man."[10] If the Anglican bishops took steps to impede the Methodist mission "to reform the nation, beginning with the Church and to spread Scriptural holiness across the land"[11] they promised to obey God instead.

Early Methodism's relationship with the COE was further complicated by the contrast that many eighteenth-century people drew between what John Wesley *said* about his loyalty to the church and what he *did* as leader of the Methodist movement. Frank Baker used the metaphor of a person in a rowboat to explain it: "While he [Wesley] kept his eyes fixed upon the

---

5. J. Wesley, *Journal and Diaries*, II:97.

6. J. Wesley, *Works* (1872), VIII:274.

7. Rack, *Works*, X:135.

8. Rack, *Works*, X:139.

9. Rack, *Works*, X:139. Emphasis original.

10. Rack, *Works*, X:155–56.

11. J. Wesley, *Works* (1872), VIII:299.

Church, he also steadily rowed in the opposite direction."[12] Baker attributed John's apparent inconsistencies to ambivalence, and John seemed to acknowledge this dilemma when he wrote: "I dare *not separate* from the Church, that I believe it would be a sin so to do. . . . [But] I believe it would be a sin *not* to vary from it [the Church] in . . . cases of necessity."[13] But to others, however, John Wesley's "ambivalence" looked more like duplicity; as one of John's critics pointed out in an open letter to the editor of the *London Magazine*: "did you not betray the Church, as Judas did his Master, with a kiss?"[14]

Anglican complaints against the Wesley brothers amounted to four specific matters: 1) "Preaching in the open air," often in other pastor's parishes without their permission; 2) "the use of extemporary prayer" even though they also loved and used the *Book of Common Prayer*; 3) employment of untrained and unapproved lay preachers; and 4) the "assignment of their place of labor within the society." The *ad hoc* and freelance character of much of the Wesleys' ministry did not fit in with the "one great chain of being" hierarchical social philosophy any better than it did hierarchical COE rules and customs.[15] The lay preachers were often an affront to social and ecclesiastical propriety; one of the Wesleys' critics remembered, for example, "the Methodist preacher came into an Anglican parish in the spirit, and with the language of a missionary going to the most ignorant heathens; and he asked the clergyman to lend him his pulpit, in order that he might instruct his parishioners for the first time in the true Gospel of Christ."[16]

None of these matters were such serious violations of church law that they merited excommunication, but the cumulative effect of them caused significant and fairly constant irritation. Practical opposition from Anglican local clergy was often so stiff that, as John confided to brother Charles, "'the clergy here hunt us down like gladiators.' But the people of all sorts receive the Word gladly."[17] The fact that John quoted the ancient poet Terence in Latin (above) so not everyone would be able to read his assessment of the COE clergy also evidenced his unwillingness to speak ill of them—at least to the general public. But the extraordinary results the Wesleys reaped by transgressing ecclesiastical propriety to take their evangelism to the unchurched made their decision to go *alfresco* an easy one. Their irritated elder

12. Baker, *John Wesley and the Church of England*, 2.

13. Baker, *John Wesley and the Church of England*, 2. Emphasis original.

14. J. Wesley, *Letters*, IV:122.

15. Harrington, *John Wesley in Company*, 134–35.

16. Lyles, *Methodism Mocked*, 28.

17. Baker, *Works*, 20:630.

brother, Samuel Wesley Jr., blamed George Whitefield and their pragmatism for it: "I am very apprehensive you would still stick to him as your dear brother, and so, though the church would *not* excommunicate you, *you would excommunicate* the church."[18]

The ecclesiastical irritation as well as a few formal complaints brought the Wesley brothers before four different Anglican bishops for tense interviews. In each case, they reached a consensus on points of doctrine, and in each case the bishop complained about the "irregularity" of the Wesleys' approach to ministry. These repeated ecclesiastical encounters were likely what caused John Wesley to modify his often repeated resolve to "live and die in the Church of England" by adding a qualifier—"*unless* I am thrust out."[19] But they were *not* thrust out and still John continued to take steps that gradually led to separation.

John Wesley's published journal self-consciously presents him as a loyal high church Anglican, who was "all my life so tenacious of every point relating to decency and order, that I should have thought the saving of souls almost a sin, if it had not been *done in a church*."[20] Whatever pragmatic steps he took in the direction away from Anglicanism, John Wesley consistently presented himself as a bridge and reconciler between the Methodists and the Church of England. For example, in 1783, just months before John's illegal ordination of a Methodist superintendent (bishop) and several priests for service in North America, John Wesley wrote, "In my journals and *Magazine*, in every possible way, I have advised the Methodists to keep to the Church. They that do this most prosper best in their souls; I have observed it long. If ever the Methodists in general were to leave the Church, I must leave them."[21]

John Wesley's intention, as well as it can be discerned from his conflicting statements and actions, was to remain within the Church of England as long as he could do so without impeding his intended mission. Functioning under an Anglican umbrella was expedient for them and also benefited the Methodists in many ways. Along with the theological and liturgical roots and credibility their COE connection gave the Methodists there were two other less obvious factors; the one was an aurora of respectability that distinguished them, in the minds of many, from outright dissenters (like the Presbyterians and Baptists). And it helped maintain their connection with a number of influential Anglican clergy, like Henry Piers, Walter Sellon,

18. Baker, *Works*, 20:661. Emphasis added.

19. Telford, *Letters of the Rev. John Wesley*, VIII:58. Emphasis original.

20. J. Wesley, *Journal and Diaries*, II:46. Emphasis original.

21. J. Wesley, *Letters*, VII:163.

William Grimshsaw, Samuel Walker, and John William Fletcher, who helped the Methodists in many ways. But John Wesley grew increasingly comfortable with departing from many of the practices and violating the policies but not the doctrines of the COE. His was a selective loyalty toward the mother church; John affirmed and supported the church he loved when that was practicable, and he took a different course when it was not.

Charles Wesley's relationship to the COE was much less ambiguous than John's. As Methodism gradually drifted away from its Anglican moorings, Charles's loyalty and adherence to the church never wavered. Where John's loyalty to the church was conditional, Charles's was not. As his brother and others took concerted steps that widened the gap between the Methodists and the Church of England, Charles stood in the gap. He balked, complained, critiqued, shouted, threatened, and sometimes stormed out of the meeting room. He stayed true to their original mission to "leaven the lump" of the Church of England and would not countenance steps that signaled a separation from the church. As Charles confided to his Anglican colleague, Dr. Chandler: "I never lost my dread of separation, or ceased to guard our societies against it. I frequently told them: 'I am your servant as long as you remain in the Church of England, but no longer. Should you forsake her, you would renounce me.'"[22] It was in this regard that Gareth Lloyd rightly described Charles Wesley as "champion of the Church-Methodist interest."[23]

Charles Wesley's fidelity to the COE put him on a collision course with the growing army of Methodist lay preachers who clamored for clergy status and sacramental privileges, both of which were contrary to Anglican church law. Charles's unqualified commitment to the Church of England also sometimes put him at odds with his brother as John became increasingly comfortable with significant departures of Anglican Church rubrics and more sympathetic toward the needs and deficiencies of the Methodist lay preachers. The tension between the Wesley brothers on this matter seems all the more ironic because it was not so much a case of them wanting different things. They both wanted the very same things, but wanted those same things differently. One of Charles's letters to his wife Sally made his priorities very clear:

> My chief concern upon earth, I said, was the prosperity of the Church of England, my next, was that of the Methodists. My third that of the Preachers. That if their interest should ever come into competition, I would give up the Preachers for the

22. Tyson, *Charles Wesley: A Reader*, 60.
23. Lloyd, *Charles Wesley and the Struggle*, 178.

good of the Methodists, and the Methodists for the good of the
whole body of the Church of England. That nothing could force
me to leave the Methodists but their leaving the Church.[24]

John Wesley was more apt to take the reverse order on Charles's three concerns; he placed the interests of the Methodists and the lay preachers ahead
of those of the church.

Two specific events figured particularly large in Methodism's separation from the COE. The first began in the 1750s, as the lay pastors agitated
for separation largely because they wanted clergy status and sacramental
authority, both of which were impossible for them under Anglican church
law. At the 1752 Methodist Annual Conference, Charles Wesley forced the
group to adopt a resolution "never to leave the communion of the Church
of England without the consent of all whose names are subjoined." The lay
preachers present either signed the loyalty oath or lost their standing among
the Methodists, and Charles's loyalty oath became a regular practice at the
Methodist Annual Conferences for the next five years.[25] But this was using
intimidation to wallpaper over the damage without repairing it. By the autumn of 1754, two lay preachers, Thomas Walsh and Charles Peronet, began
administering communion and when they were not immediately censored
for it three more lay preachers followed their example. A firestorm of controversy followed with heated letters passing between the Wesley brothers,
and with Charles marshaling support from "the Church Methodist" faction
to curtail the efforts of the lay preachers, who now numbered more than
sixty.

The Annual Conference of 1755 spent seven or eight sessions in "conversation" about the church and separation. John Wesley wistfully summarized the event in this journal: "Whatever was advanced on one side or the
other was seriously and calmly considered; and on the third day we were
all fully agreed in that general conclusion—that whether [separation] was
lawful or not, it was in no ways *expedient*."[26] Whatever Charles might have
said at the conference it is hard to imagine it was "calmly considered." He
likely chafed at the word "expedient" since he confided in a letter to Lady
Huntingdon: "It seems as if God was warning me to prepare for some great
change. What He does with me or by me I know not now, and never see
two steps before me."[27] Charles also wrote several very irritable letters to his

24. Charles's Manuscript Letter, quoted by Lloyd, *Charles Wesley and the Struggle*,
170.

25. Baker, *John Wesley and the Church of England*, 160–61.

26. J. Wesley, *Journal and Diaries*, IV:10. Emphasis added.

27. Baker, *John Wesley and the Church of England*, 162.

exasperated brother John, who replied: "Do you not understand that they all promised by T. Walsh not to administer [communion] even among themselves? I think that is a huge point given up perhaps more than they could give up with a clear conscience. . . . The practical conclusion was, 'not to separate from the Church? Did we not all agree in this? Surely either you or I must have been asleep, or we could not differ so widely in a matter of fact.'"[28]

The inner dynamics of the sacramental controversy of the 1750s were rooted in the tension between Anglican church order—which stipulated only ordained clergy could administer the sacraments and what the lay preachers perceived to be their proper status and the genuine needs of the Methodist people. Methodist "rules" committed the people to using "the means of grace," and this took them to their parish churches to receive the Lord's Supper but when they went to the church they were often made to feel unwelcome. Why should the Methodists endure weekly ridicule at the COE when they had preachers of their own? The conversation was further complicated by issues of class; many of the Anglican clergy could not accept the often uneducated and lower-class Methodist lay preachers as worthy colleagues, and some of their congregants felt the same way. The lay pastors saw themselves doing the same work as their ordained colleagues and quite often more of it. It seemed right to them that they should enjoy equal status and prerogatives. This is a conversation that has been renewed very recently as the United Methodist Church and other Wesleyan denominations have begun to rely more and more on the services of licensed lay pastors and bivocational ministers. These internal ecclesiastical tensions burst upon the international scene in 1784, when John Wesley illegally ordained a Methodist bishop and several clergy for service in North America.

The planting of Methodism in America was chiefly the work of Irish immigrants like Barbara Ruckle Heck, Philip Embury, and Robert Strawbridge, who fled hardship and persecution and came to America for a new start in life. They brought their Methodism with them and their contributions were soon supplemented by British colonialist soldiers, like Captain Webb, and their many new converts. Following an urgent request from the Methodist Society that met in a sail rigging loft in New York City in 1768, John Wesley tried to send missionary pastors to the struggling fellowship. His efforts met with varying degrees of success but came to an utter standstill when "the war of the American Rebellion" broke out in 1776 and almost all of the British loyalists among the clergy returned to England or made their way to Canada. The only exception to this exodus of Methodist preachers was Francis Asbury, who spent most of the war years hiding out in rural

---

28. Baker, *Works*, 20:561.

Maryland. After the war, Asbury's prodigious efforts rebuilt the Methodist movement in America to more than 15,000 members, but as a lay pastor he was unable to administer the sacraments to his growing flock. Once again, the Methodists were faced with the dilemma of not receiving the sacraments, or having their sacraments administered by a layman. When no ordained clergy could be cajoled into coming to America, John Wesley went through a series of increasingly desperate and unsuccessful schemes to secure ordination for a few of his lay preachers who were willing to go to America.

During this same period, Wesley studied church history and polity with an eye to finding a creative solution to the Methodist dilemma in

*Thomas Coke, **President of the Methodist Conference**, by a contemporary artist, from Wikimedia (public domain)*

America. When John read *The Irenicum: A Weapon Salve for the Church's Wounds* (1659) by Bishop Edward Stillingfleet, a closed door was opened in his thinking. Stillingfleet argued that no form of church government, including the episcopacy, was prescribed by the New Testament. Since Stillingfleet believed that no particular church polity was singularly truly ordained by God, the best approach to church government was one that bore the most spiritual fruit for the people of God. John Wesley's own copy of *The Irenicum* was inscribed in his handwriting: "I think he fully proves his point, J.W. 1760."[29] John also read Peter King's *Enquiry into the Constitution, Discipline, Unity, and Worship of the Primitive Church* (1691) soon thereafter. John Wesley soon came to the conclusion "that bishops and presbyters are (essentially) the same order, and that originally every Christian congregation was a church independent on all others."[30] Mulling over these readings, in the context of his many failed attempts at securing ordination for Methodist pastors for America, provided the impetus for John Wesley's "creative solution" to the sacramental dilemma.

At 5 a.m. on September 1, 1784, John Wesley called a special meeting at the home of Dr. John Castleman in Bristol. The time and location gave the gathering a clandestine feel, and the fact that Charles Wesley, who was

29. Baker, *John Wesley and the Church of England*, 145–46.

30. J. Wesley, *Journal and Diaries*, III:112.

in Bristol at the time, was not invited confirms it. Before a small and hand-picked group, John Wesley "appointed" Dr. Thomas Coke (1747–1814), who was a priest in the Church of England, to be a Methodist "superintendent" for America. Two lay pastors, Richard Watson and Thomas Vassey, were also "appointed" to be priests to serve the American Methodists. Soon these three men were on their way to America, where Dr. Coke "ordained" Francis Asbury as a "bishop." In John Wesley's journal and letters these men were "appointed" and Coke and Asbury were named "superintendents." But in the mind of the Francis Asbury and American Methodists they were "ordained" clergy, and with the bishops the Americans received a Methodist ecclesiastical tradition of their own.

Charles Wesley learned of the clandestine ordinations two months after the event through private correspondence with one of his Bristol friends. "I am thunderstruck," Charles explained, "I can hardly believe it!"[31] However utterly surprised he was, Charles was not caught without words for the occasion. He fired off several poison-pen letters to his brother John and composed two volumes of sad and angry hymns. Charles's disappointment outlasted his anger, however, and eight months later it was with sadness he described the event to his Anglican friend, Dr. Chandler: "I can scarce yet believe it, that, in his eighty-second year, my Brother, my old intimate friend and companion, should have assumed the Episcopal Character, ordained Elders, Consecrated a Bishop, and send him to ordain our lay-preachers in America."[32] "He never gave me a hint of his intention," Charles wrote with a sense of betrayal, "How was he surprised into so rash an action? He certainly persuaded himself that it was right."[33] Charles's feelings of betrayal and exclusion were real enough, but John's actions were *not* rash; they were well considered and based on research that he began almost twenty years before.

Borrowing a phrase from his childhood friend, William Murray, who became Lord Mansfield, Chief Justice of England, Charles concluded, "Ordination is separation."[34] It was at this point that Charles announced that his fifty-year partnership in ministry with his brother John was over. Charles continued to serve the Methodist congregations he had helped build in London, but he ceased traveling as an itinerant and no longer worked in concert with his brother: "Thus our Partnership here is dissolved, but not our Friendship. I have taken him for better or worse, till death do us part;

---

31. Tyson, "Charles Wesley and the Church of England," 482.
32. Tyson, *Charles Wesley: A Reader*, 60.
33. Tyson, *Charles Wesley: A Reader*, 60.
34. Tyson, *Charles Wesley: A Reader*, 60.

or rather, re-united us in love inseparable. I have lived on earth a little too long—who have lived to see this evil day."[35] While John quibbled with Charles as to whether he had actually separated from the church or not, it was clear to both men that John's ordinations *had* separated him from his brother and from the church Methodists. Ordination was, indeed, separation.

FOR FURTHER CONSIDERATION:

1. The Wesley brothers valued many of the same things—the church, the Methodists, and the preachers—but they valued them differently. Did this difference need to end in impasse?

2. How can people of faith work through the process of having different and sometimes conflicting priorities?

3. Charles Wesley's loyalty to the church was unmixed, whereas John gave the church a "qualified commitment." What sort of commitment should one have towards the church? How does one sort out where commitment ends?

4. There is at the heart of this controversy a tension between spiritual ideals and ecclesiastical pragmatism. How can we navigate our way between those two ideas?

5. John Wesley conducted his ministry in many ways that separated him (tacitly) from the Church of England, and yet he thought he could and did avoid schism. Was that reasonable? Are there lessons here for modern Methodists and other Christians?

35. Tyson, *Charles Wesley: A Reader*, 60.

Chapter 15

"Your Daughters Shall Prophesy"
Controversy over Women's Preaching and Leadership

WOMEN ENROLLED IN EARLY Methodist classes and bands two or three times more frequently than men. The attraction Methodism held for eighteenth-century women varied, but the sense of value, purpose, and spiritual equality they found among there were certainly significant factors. The affirmation of their "spiritual equality," however, did not result in equal treatment or opportunities for them. New Testament passages like "Let your women keep silence in the churches: for it is not permitted unto them to speak" (1 Cor 14:35) and "I suffer not a woman to teach, nor to usurp authority over the man, but to be in silence" (1 Tim 2:12), when added to the social restrictions of the Georgian era, effectively silenced women when it came to public preaching and religious leadership.

Female preachers were not unknown in eighteenth-century England, but they were generally associated with spiritualistic "fringe groups" who, under the immediacy of the Spirit, allowed females to preach and lead. Women preachers were more often considered an affront to social decorum and ecclesiastical order, as well as an utter curiosity. English playwright and author Dr. Samuel Johnson (1709–84) voiced the disdain associated with female preachers when he quipped to his friend Boswell: "Sir, a woman's preaching is like a dog's walking on it's hind legs. It is not done well; but you are surprised to find it done at all."[1]

Women's public leadership in Methodism was an outgrowth of their substantial roles in the more private world of classes, bands, and societies.

---

1. Boswell, *Life of Samuel Johnson*, 74.

Just as eighteenth-century women enjoyed much greater freedom and opportunities in domestic and nonpublic spheres of activity,[2] so also did early Methodist women enjoy more freedom and opportunity in their Methodist small groups than they did in their Anglican churches. As John Wesley explained, "Many were surprised when I told them, 'The very design of the love feast is free and familiar conversation, in which every man, yea, every woman, has liberty to speak whatever may be to the glory of God.'"[3] Earlier that same year, John reported: "After preaching at the Foundry in the evening, I met the bands as usual. While a poor woman was speaking a few artless words out of the fullness of her heart, a fire kindled and ran, as flame among the stubble, through the hearts of almost all that heard; so, when God is pleased to work, it matters not how weak or how mean ["common"] the instrument."[4]

The gradual emergence of female preachers in early Methodism went through three discernable phases. The first of these was "the clandestine phase" in which pious and talented women gradually extended the boundaries of the testifying and exhorting that was acceptable for them in the Methodist small groups. John Wesley was present during one of these spontaneous testimonies by a young woman in Wales, and reported:

> Two clergymen were there besides me, and the house was full of people. But she could not refrain from declaring before them all what God had done for her soul. And the words that came from the heart went to the heart. I scarce ever heard such *a preacher* before. All were in tears round her, high and low [class people]; for there was no resisting the Spirit by which she spoke.[5]

Several things were notable in Wesley's report: the woman's testimony was perceived to be a spontaneous event prompted by the Holy Spirit. Since the event occurred in the "nonpublic" venue of a Methodist Society meeting and not in "a church," it did not (in the strictest sense of the words) violate the prohibition of 1 Corinthians 14:34: "Let your women keep silence *in the churches*." The urgency with which the Spirit-led speaking moment came upon the unnamed woman meant she did not seek and was not required to ask permission from the male clergy who were present, because her speaking was not viewed as a sermon (which would have been prohibited). In this case, the various New Testament passages about women *prophesying* (Acts 2:18; 21:8–9; 1 Cor 11:5) took precedent over those texts that demanded

2. See Klein, "Gender," 97–109.

3. J. Wesley, *Journal and Diaries*, IV:336.

4. J. Wesley, *Journal and Diaries*, IV:303.

5. J. Wesley, *Journal and Diaries*, III:128.

their silence. These spontaneous events offered a pattern for the Methodists to find exceptions to the ordinary prohibitions against women preaching; women could "speak" or "testify" spontaneously when they were led by the Holy Spirit. They could also speak, and indeed were *expected* to speak, in the nonpublic world of Methodist classes, bands, and societies.

Early Methodist women, like Sarah Crosby (1729–1804), thrived on these Methodist fellowship opportunities and grew spiritually through them. After seven years of fellowship and the friendship of other remarkable Methodist women, including Sarah Ryan, Mary Clark, and Mary Bosanquet, Ms. Crosby became a class leader.[6] Another three years passed as Sarah Crosby continued to grow in her faith and she grew in certainty about her own call to preach. The first occasion was on February 1, 1761, and her powerful witness brought more than 200 people to Ms. Crosby's class meeting. She reported: "I was not sure whether it was right for me to exhort in so public a manner, and yet I saw it impossible to meet all these people by way of speaking particularly to each individual. I, therefore, gave out a hymn, and prayed, and told them part of what the Lord had done for myself, persuading them to flee from all sin."[7] Because of her concern about the propriety of her speaking, Sarah penned an inquiry to John Wesley. But before she received Wesley's reply, she found herself in a similar situation once again, and in that second incident she felt the leading of the Lord so powerfully that her inner turmoil about public speaking melted away: "My soul was much comforted in speaking to the people, as my Lord has removed all my scruples respecting my acting thus publically."[8]

John Wesley's written reply arrived the next day: "Hitherto, I think you have not gone too far," he wrote, "you could not well do less."[9] But Wesley was concerned that her first preaching event might lead to other events (which it already had). He was also concerned that her "speaking" might be misconstrued as "preaching." Wesley advised: "If you do more when you meet [the Band] again, tell them simply, 'You lay me under a great difficulty. The Methodists do not allow women preachers. Neither do I take upon me any such a character. But I will just . . . tell you what is in my heart.' This will in a great measure obviate the grand objection."[10] Once Sarah Crosby announced the disclaimer: "the Methodists do not allow women preachers,"

---

6. "Sarah Crosby Woman Preacher."

7. Chilcote, *John Wesley and the Women Preachers*, 120.

8. Chilcote, *John Wesley and the Women Preachers*, 122.

9. Campbell, *Works*, 20:241.

10. Campbell, *Works*, 27:242.

and made it clear that she was "speaking" and *not really* preaching, she was free to address her Methodist band or society.

The small crack Sarah Crosby opened in the stained-glass ceiling that kept women from progressing upward toward preaching was both an example and precedent. But when Grace Walton followed Sarah's example, just five months later, she received a less sympathetic response from John Wesley. "If a few more persons came in when you are meeting, you may either enlarge four or five minutes on a question you had, or give a short exhortation (perhaps five or six minutes) and then sing and pray," he wrote. "This is going as far as I think any woman should do; for the words of the apostle are clear."[11] Wesley cited 1 Timothy 2:11–12 as support for his more restrictive response to Grace Walton: "I suffer not a woman to teach in a congregation nor assert authority over the man."

John Wesley's personal ambivalence was evident in the contrasting advice he offered to Sarah Crosby and Grace Walton. It showed that he was trying to embrace the new thing God was doing, namely the calling of female preachers among the Methodists, while simultaneously holding fast to the old strictures and customs. It was a classic example of trying to put "new wine in old wine skins" (Mark 2:22), and as Jesus pointed out, new wine belongs in *new* wine skins because the old structures cannot contain the new thing God is doing. This realization led to "phase two" of the emergence of female preachers among the Methodists based on their new standing as having "extraordinary call."[12] Wesley and the Methodists found a way to reconcile themselves to what they believed to be the Bible's prohibitions and yet embrace the belief that these were called by God to preach, which allowed them to reap the tremendous fruit that accompanied their preaching. As a prophetic event of the Holy Spirit, the women's "extraordinary call" made the traditional prohibitions and ecclesiastical restrictions against female preaching seem less appropriate and the undeniable fruits of their efforts made it seem necessary. If God was honoring the efforts of female preachers, why shouldn't the Methodists do the same?

The question of what constituted an authentic "call to preach" was addressed at the Methodist Conference of 1746. The "Minutes" established three main criteria by which a person's call was to be evaluated: (1) "Do they know in whom they have believed?"—that is to say: Do they *know* God, or do they merely *know about* God? (2) "Have they gifts as well as graces for the work?" And then the pragmatic question: (3) "Have they success?" Hence, "as long as these three marks undeniably concur in any we allow *him* to be

---

11. Campbell, *Works*, 27:275.

12. Chilcote, *John Wesley and Women Preachers*, 141–82. Emphasis mine.

called to preach."[13] Notably, the official "Minutes" assumed these "marks" would "allow *him* to be called to preach" but there is no consideration that the preacher might be "a her." In almost every instance of women preaching, however, it was the third "mark"—their success—that swung the balance in *her* favor. When a woman's preaching bore overwhelmingly positive fruit, her "call" to preach simply could not be doubted or ignored.

John Wesley seemed to recognize how futile it was to distinguish between women "speaking" or "testifying" and women "preaching." It was an exercise in semantics, which did not convince many people and likely did not satisfy Wesley himself. This dilemma sent him back to the Bible and his study showed him a proliferation of speaking and teaching offices in the primitive church. But when the church became a public institution during Emperor Constantine's reign, "It soon grew common for one man to take whole charge of a congregation, in order to engross the whole pay. Hence, the same person acted as priest and prophet, as pastor and evangelist. And this gradually spread more and more throughout the whole Christian church."[14] Wesley's new pragmatic approach to women's right to preach was reflected in his commentary on 1 Corinthians 14:34–35 where the text's "Let you women be silent in the churches" included an exception: women should be silent "*unless they are under an extraordinary impulse of the Spirit.* For in other cases, 'it is not permitted them to speak.'—by way of teaching in publick [sic.] assemblies. 'But to be in subjection'—to the man whose proper office it is lead and instruct the congregation.'"[15] The emergence of female preachers in the life of early Methodism reshaped John Wesley's interpretation of the Bible and opened the avenue of their "extraordinary call" by the Holy Spirit. John Wesley found a second "work-around" for his dilemma of Methodist women preachers. He added the distinction between the prohibitive ecclesiastical "ordinary rule," and the spiritually spontaneous "extraordinary call" was added to the earlier distinction between the private world of Methodist small groups and

Mary Bosanquet Fletcher, **unknown artist. Public domain.**

13. Rack, *Works*, X:177–78.

14. J. Wesley, *Sermons*, IV:77.

15. J. Wesley, *Explanatory Notes*, 440 (emphasis original); Wesley's comment on 1 Corinthians 14:34.

public preaching. Hence, the Methodists could say with the other eighteenth-century Anglicans: "We have a rule against women's preaching," while they also acknowledged that God the Holy Spirit works in "extraordinary" ways that break the boundaries set by any general rule.

The third and last phase of the emergence of early Methodist female preachers could be called "normalizing the extraordinary call." Here the defining moment was the correspondence between John Wesley and Ms. Mary Bosanquet (1739–1815). In 1771, Mary wrote Wesley a very long letter explaining her call to "do all I can for God," which ultimately led to her substituting for a male lay preacher in his absence. She spoke with utterly remarkable results. Things had changed during the decade separating Sarah Crosby's inquiry of 1761 and Mary Bosanquet's epistle. Sarah wrote seeking John Wesley's permission and approval, but Mary had already made up her mind. Mary was going to preach whenever and wherever God the Holy Spirit called her to do so. She wrote to *inform* John Wesley and to court his approval, *not* to ask his permission.

The gradual emergence and acceptance of the idea that women could and did have an authentic but "extraordinary call" to preach formed the basis for Mary's case. In a succinct and tightly reasoned fashion, Ms. Bosanquet wrote a theological apology for women's right to preach and demolished a dozen of the objections often brought against it. John Wesley's reply to Mary Bosanquet signaled a change in him as well; rather than looking for ways to limit her preaching, as he did with Sarah Crosby or Grace Walton, Wesley embraced Mary's call to preach and put it on par with that of his male lay preachers. "I think the strength of the cause rests here, on your having an *extraordinary call*," he wrote, "so, I am persuaded, has every one of our Lay Preachers; otherwise I could not countenance his preaching at all."[16] All told, Mary Bosanquet Fletcher had a powerful preaching ministry that spanned four decades.

Careful scholarship by Paul Chilcote identified more than forty female Methodist preachers who served Methodism during John Wesley's lifetime.[17] Each of these women was acknowledged to have an "extraordinary call" to preach but none of them had their preaching formalized by licensing or ordination. This raises the obvious question: How many "extraordinary calls" were needed till women's ministry could be made "ordinary?" The apparent answer was: "quite a few more." John Wesley's support for the preaching ministry of females was short-lived. When Wesley named the "legal 100

---

16. J. Wesley, *Letters*, V:2. Emphasis original.
17. Chilcote, *She Offered Them Christ*, 106–9.

preachers"[18] who formed the leadership of the British Methodist Conference that succeeded him in leadership upon his death, not one woman was among them. The Conference's subsequent actions indicated they did not share John Wesley's openness to the call of female preachers. In 1803, for example, the British Methodist Conference reacted to the extraordinary impact of Mary Britt Taft's evangelism by raising the question of whether or not women should preach. Despite the obvious fruits of her ministry, their reply was almost entirely negative. The entirely male annual conference allowed that a woman *could* have an "extraordinary call" to preach, but the male clergy would judge the authenticity of her call and should they deign to authorize it "she should address, in general, *her own sex, and those only*."[19]

The steps began in 1803 effectively ended female preaching in the Wesleyan Methodist Connexion. Soon revivalist-minded British Methodists formed spin-off groups like the Primitive Methodists (1807) and the Bible Christians (1807) who were intent upon holding fast the movement's original identity. They both welcomed female preachers and ordained them. The Salvation Army formed in 1865 by former Methodists William and Catherine Booth to recover Methodism's urban mission, and they too offered women the equivalent of full ordination. But the main British Wesleyan Methodist Church first ordained women as deacons in 1896, and finally granted women full ordination in 1974.

In its early decades, American Methodism was profoundly shaped by women who, as "Mothers in Israel," used and extended their domestic roles into avenues of unpaid but significant ministry (see chapter 7 above). Catherine Brekus described the severe prejudice faced by women who felt called to preach the gospel or lead in worship. This is illustrated by the assessment made by one of their male clergy colleagues, who opined, "Christian women who invited men to stare at them in public, even to proclaim the gospel, were no better than prostitutes."[20] Harriet Livermore (1788–1868), "the best known female

James Barton Longacre, *Harriet Livermore* (**1827**). **The image is a stipple engraving on paper, 12.7 cm x 8.6 cm, in the National Portrait Gallery, the Smithsonian Institution, where it is object no. NPG.2018.17 (open access).**

18. J. Wesley, *Works of John Wesley*, XIII:249–50.

19. Chilcote, *She Offered Them Christ*, 106–9. Emphasis original.

20. Brekus, "Female Preaching," 21.

preacher of her day," was a lightning rod for America's double-mindedness about the capacity of religious women. She was described by some as "bold and shameless," while to others she was "the instrument of God."[21] Harriet was immortalized in John Greenleaf Whittier's poem "Snow Bound": "A woman tropical, intense/In thought and act, in soul and sense,/She blended in a like degree/The vixen and the devotee."[22] Whittier's description of Ms. Livermore as "Vixen and [religious] devotee" expressed well the dichotomy faced by female preachers.

Despite prejudice and opposition, female preachers emerged in American Methodism during the revivalist era by drawing upon the *ad hoc,* Spirit-directed "prophetic" model; they, too, evidenced "the extraordinary call." For this reason, they often spoke, or seemed to speak, extemporaneously, without formal preparation, status, or ordination. They were also without ordination's benefits and recognition. As the Methodist Episcopal Church strove to gain legitimacy among the American middle and upper classes, women preachers faced increased opposition. The Methodist Protestant Church (1828), the Wesleyan Methodist Church (1841), and the Free Methodist Church (1860), all of whom left the Methodist Episcopal Church (MEC) during the revivalist period for a variety of reasons, had in common greater openness to women preachers than their parent body.

Second Great Awakening revivalism, as epitomized by Charles Finney (1792–1875) and popularized in his influential *Lectures on Revivals of Religion* (1835), combined revivalist concerns about saving "souls" with social reform.[23] Finney's "new measures" revivalism opened greater opportunities for women by encouraging women to lead out in prayer, and sometimes to speak ("testify") before "promiscuous" audiences of women and men.[24] His evangelistic ministry and presidency at Oberlin College birthed a multitude of abolitionist and benevolent societies in which Christian women expanded their "domestic" roles into social service opportunities. Endemic to revivalism, particularly the Wesleyan toned revivalism of Charles Finney, was the interconnection of revivalism and social reform.[25] In Wesleyan varieties of revivalism, the bridge between personal and social salvation was sanctification—the traditional Wesleyan emphasis upon "holiness of heart *and* life." Hence, divinely "called" Methodist women, like Mary Morgan Mason, Laura Smith Haviland, Mary Clarke Nind (all of whom we will meet

21. Brekus, "Female Preaching," 20.
22. Whittier, "Snow Bound," lines 531–35.
23. See "Evangelical Origins of Social Christianity," in Smith, *Revivalism*, 148–63.
24. Finney, *Lectures*, 29, 77, 128, 148.
25. Smith, *Revivalism*, 148–63.

in chapter 17 as "Mothers in Israel"), Frances Willard, and many others, entered full-time Christian ministry through the avenue of service and social reform.

Francis Willard (1839–98) was raised as nominal Methodist, in Evanston, Illinois. But during a near-fatal illness in her late teens she had a dramatic religious experience that deepened her resolve: "If God lets me get well I'll try to be a Christian girl," Frances later confided to her journal.[26] Following her attendance at a December 1859 revival led by MEC Bishop Matthew Simpson, she made a profession of faith and was received into probationary membership in the MEC. She was baptized into full membership a year later. Frances continued her education at North Western Female College, and after teaching for the next nine years, Ms. Willard intensified her focus on "the cause of woman."[27] In 1868, Frances read several biographies of early Methodist women as well as *A Guide to Holiness* by Phoebe Palmer, whom she met in the winter of 1866.[28] Ms. Willard's friendship with Phoebe Palmer deepened her passion for Christian service and social reform. In 1874, she was instrumental in the establishment of the Women's Christian Temperance Union (WCTU), and under Frances Willard's able leadership the WCTU became a "do it all" institution that strove for the equality and enablement of all people.

Artist unknown, *Frances Willard,* **a print from the George Grantham Bain Collection (Library of Congress), made from the original negative 5" x 7," LC-B2- 598–10, in Library of Congress Prints and Photographs Division Washington, D.C. 20540 USA**

Frances Willard was elected as a lay delegate to the 1888 MEC General Conference but was prevented from being seated among the voting delegates, along with four other prominent Methodist women, because the MEC *Discipline* specified "lay*men*" could attend, but not lay*women*. In her autobiography Ms. Willard described her feeling of betrayal by quoting Shakespeare's famous line from *Julius Caesar*: "Once more it was a case of *Et tu Brute!* 'Thou too, Brutus!' That the bishops should have 'left us lamenting,' grieved me, but when the lay delegates did the same, I said in my heart, 'Once more the action of my fellow mortals weans me from love of life, and by so doing they have doubtless helped me more than their generosity of

26. Gifford, "'My Own Methodist Hive,'" 81.

27. Gifford, "'My Own Methodist Hive,'" 87.

28. Willard, *Glimpses of Fifty Years*, 624–25.

action could possibly have done."[29] Not only did Willard resolve to use her disappointment as grist for her own spiritual growth, she found in it the impetus to press on for the full equality of women.[30] She wrote, "I lost no sleep and wasted no tears over the curious transaction, and I confidently predict that we five women, whose election was thus disavowed, will have more enviable places in history than any who opposed us on those memorable days. Of them it will be written . . . that they committed an injustice; of us, only that we endured it."[31]

Frances Willard took the long view of those hurtful events and tried to put them in a more hopeful context: "The champions of equality made a splendid record, of which they will be prouder with each added year. They are forerunners of that grander, because more equitable, polity that shall yet glorify our Methodism when in her law, as in Christ's gospel, there shall be 'Neither male nor female.'"[32] Ms. Willard continued to use her international platform as president of the WCTU (1879–91) to push for equality and enablement. In 1904, laywomen *were* seated as delegates at the MEC General Conference, but without voice or vote. It was not until 1914, just six years ahead of women's suffrage, that women were granted full and equal rights as MEC lay delegates.

P. S. Duval, *Mrs. Jarena Lee* (1849), a lithographic print made from the life portrait by A. Huffy. From the frontispiece of Jarena Lee's autobiography, *Religious Experience and Journal of Mrs. Jarena Lee*, privately published by the author in Philadelphia (1849). In the Library of Congress Prints and Photographs Division, No. LC-USZ62–42044, Washington, DC, 20540.

The Second Great Awakening also opened preaching opportunities for gifted women like the African Methodist Episcopal evangelist Jarena Lee (1783–1855), Methodist Protestant frontier circuit rider Helenor Davisson (1823–76), holiness evangelist Phoebe Palmer (1797–1874), and black WCTU evangelist and social activist Amanda Berry Smith (1831–1915). Each of these women had remarkable preaching ministries but were denied ordination. Davisson was ordained as a transitional deacon by the Methodist Protestants of Indiana, arguably the first woman formally ordained by the Methodists, only to have her credentials revoked by

29. Willard, *Glimpses of Fifty Years*, 621.

30. Editors of Encyclopaedia Britannica, "Frances Willard."

31. Willard, *Glimpses of Fifty Years*, 621.

32. Willard, *Glimpses of Fifty Years*, 621.

the MP General Conference. When Jerena Lee pressed AMEZ Bishop Richard Allen for formal status, she was first ignored and finally licensed as an "exhorter." Sally Thompson was charged with "insubordination" and excommunicated by the Methodist Episcopal Church in 1830.[33] In 1835, Mrs. Palmer began conducting "Tuesday meetings for the promotion of holiness"[34] in her New York City home, and she was a director at the Five Points Mission. During the Methodist Centennial she emerged as "the most influential woman in the largest, fastest-growing religious group in America. At her instigation, missions began, camp meetings evangelized, and an estimated 25,000 Americans converted."[35] She conducted more than 300 holiness crusades, on both sides of the Atlantic, without formal credentials in the MEC.

Artist unknown, *Mrs. Phoebe Palmer* (circa 1855), a lithographic print in the frontispiece of her *Incidental Illustrations of the Economy of Holiness: Its Doctrines and Duties* (Boston, Henry V. Degen, 1855).

The path trod by those American women who resolved to work *within* the Methodist Episcopal Church and to strive for equal opportunities and ordained status was a long and difficult one. It began with the ministry of Margaret ("Maggie") Newton Van Cott (1830–1914). Margaret was born in New York City and had a dramatic religious conversion at the historic John's Street Methodist Church; she heard a voice calling upon her "to turn her life over to the Lord."[36] She taught Sunday School at John's Street, and engaged in evangelistic social work at Palmer's Five Points Mission. In 1866, she spoke in a religious meeting at a school house with great effect. This was the first of many similar opportunities in which Ms. Van Cott violated the traditional "private/public" distinction regarding Methodist women's "speaking." When confronted about her violation of ecclesiastical decorum by a male Methodist minister, she retorted,

Artist unknown, *Mrs. Margaret Newton Van Cott* (circa 1870), a lithographic print in *The Life and Labors of Mrs. Margaret Newton Van Cott*, by John O. Foster (Cincinnati: Hitchcock & Walden, 1872), public domain.

33. Richey et al., *Methodist Experience*, II:198–204.

34. Richey et al., *Methodist Experience*, II:198–204.

35. Richey et al., *Methodist Experience*, II:198–204.

36 "Margaret Newton Van Cott," 2.

"I believe my tongue is my own . . . and I will use it when I please, where I please, and as I please."[37]

In September 1868, Margaret van Cott was given an exhorter's license, and then a year later, the Methodist Quarterly Conference Stone Ridge, Ellenville, New York, issued her license to preach. She was the first woman to receive an official license to preach from the MEC.[38] The first "round" of her assigned circuit brought more than 500 people to faith, but in 1874 she was refused ordination by the MEC Annual Conference. Failing to secure MEC ordination did not end her ministry. Like so many talented women before her, Maggie became a noncredentialed itinerant evangelist. Margaret Newton Van Cott preached nearly 10,000 evangelistic meetings between 1866 and 1912, to great effect.[39]

Remarkably similar was the pilgrimage of Anna Howard Shaw (1847–1919). British born, her family relocated to the Michigan frontier in 1859, where from an early age she realized she was called by God to preach. Acting upon her "call to preach," Anna Shaw attended Albion College (1873),

and Boston University School of Theology (1876). Despite earning the highest score on the MEC ordination exam, Anna Howard Shaw (along with Ann Oliver) was denied ordination in 1880. She withdrew from the MEC and was granted ordination in the Methodist Protestant Church (MPC) so that she could more fully serve her two Methodist congregations in East Dennis, Massachusetts. Rev. Shaw's own disappointment, however, was echoed in her recounting of the saga of Frances E. Willard, with whom she was "closely associated in work and affection."[40] Ms. Willard "always longed to be ordained and would have been one of the most brilliant and convincing preachers of all history. Although unmistakably destined by God as a great spiritual leader, she was never authorized by man to fulfill this mission, and was not considered worthy even to sit in the high councils of the church she had chosen."[41] In a presentation she gave on women in ministry,

Artist unknown, *Anna Howard Shaw* (circa 1912), from A History of Women's Suffrage, Rochester, Charles Mann (1922), by Susan B. Anthony, public domain.

---

37. "Margaret Newton Van Cott," 2.

38. "Margaret Newton Van Cott," 2.

39. "Margaret Newton Van Cott," 2.

40. Shaw, *Story of a Pioneer*, 96.

41. Chilcote, *Methodist Defense of Women*, 207.

Dr. Anna Shaw prophetically described the path that lay ahead for women who sought ordination in mainline, male-denominated Christian churches:

> It will require many years of loyal and unflagging service in barren and untried field before women will be able to prove to cold and skeptical denominations their capabilities for the ministry. Not only will they have to do the work as well as men, but they will be compelled to prove themselves superior before just recognition will be accorded them. They had to stand this crucial test in every other department of the world's work, and the church will prove no exception to the rule. The last of the learned professions to accord to women equal opportunities with men will be the ministry, and yet the church is founded upon the sublime declaration, "God is no respecter of persons" [Acts 14:34], and "there is neither male nor female, for you are all one in Christ Jesus the Lord" [Gal 3:28].[42]

Anna Oliver (1840–92), another female trail-blazer, was born and baptized as "Vivianna Olivia Snowden." Viviana changed her name to Anna Oliver when she decided to enter into ministry in order to spare her family great embarrassment.[43] Anna earned a BA and MA from Rutgers Female College in New Jersey, and in 1868, in the wake of the Civil War, went south to teach black children, where she experienced racial prejudice through her efforts among people of African descent as well as gender prejudice focused against her by the mission agency that paid her one-half the salary received by her male colleagues. After resigning in protest, she studied in the theology department at Oberlin (1873) and Boston University School of Theology, graduating with a BD in 1876. After serving the MEC in Passaic, New Jersey, she became pastor at the MEC in Brooklyn (1879).[44]

Her Methodist Quarterly Conference recommended Anna Oliver for Deacons Orders in 1880, but Bishop Andrews refused to allow her name to be put into nomination (along with that of Anna Howard Shaw). She was severely criticized and verbally attacked for pursuing her call to ordained ministry. Her Brooklyn church divided over the contention, and a progressive group of laity purchased nearby Wesley MEC when it went up for sale at auction. They reorganized that church under Five Principles that included "gender inclusiveness," and renamed themselves the Willobughby Church; they also retained Rev. Anna Oliver as their pastor. Instead of leaving the

42. Chilcote, *Methodist Defense of Women*, 208–9.
43. Rowe, "Evangelism and Social Reform," 117.
44. Rowe, "Evangelism and Social Reform," 121.

MCE, however, Oliver fought unsuccessfully to have all gender-specific language removed from the ordination requirements in the MEC *Book of Discipline*. When Willobughby Church was forced to close in 1883, Rev. Oliver continued to preach throughout New York City; she was also active in the WCTU and in the cause of women's suffrage.[45] Her friend and colleague Dr. Anna Howard Shaw eulogized her at the 1893 Women's Suffrage Association Convention:

> The Rev. Anna Oliver [was] the first woman to enter the theological department of Boston University. She was much beloved by her class. She was a devoted Christian, eminently orthodox, and a very good worker in all lines of religious effort. . . . She was denied ordination by Bishop Andrews. Our claims were carried to the General Conference in Cincinnati, and the Methodist Episcopal Church denied ordination to the two women whom it had graduated in its schools and upon whom it conferred the degree of bachelor of divinity. It not only did this, but it made a step backwards; it took away from us the licenses to preach which had been granted to Miss Oliver for four years and to myself for eight years. . . .
>
> Miss Oliver was not only the minister and the minister's wife, but she started at least a dozen reforms and undertook to carry them all out. She was attacked by that influential Methodist paper, the Christian Advocate, edited by Rev. Dr. James M. Buckley, who declared that he would destroy her influence in the church, and so with that great organ behind him he attacked her. She had that to fight, the world to fight, and the devil to fight, and she broke down. She went abroad to recover, but came home only to die.[46]

Artist unknown, *Dr. Georgia Harkness*, photo on the cover of the November 1953 issue of Pulpit Digest, public domain.

Georgia Harkness (1891–1974) was the most prominent female theologian of the twentieth century, and a strong advocate for the ordination of women in the MEC. After a brief career in public education, she entered Boston University, where

45. Rowe, "Evangelism and Social Reform," 130–31.
46. Stanton, *History of Women's Suffrage*, IV:206–7.

she was encouraged not to enter the BD program, so she earned an MA and PhD in systematic theology instead.[47] Dr. Harkness pursued a stellar career in theological education at Garrett (1939–50) and Pacific School of Religion (1950–61). Harkness was, as her biographer Rosemary Skinner Keller described her, "a folk theologian." She was a theologian of the people who had, in Georgia's own words, the ability "to make theology understandable to people."[48] The defining moment of her illustrious career came in 1924 as Dr. Georgia Harkness addressed the MEC General Conference on the topic of the full ordination of women.

The pioneering work of Madeline Southard (1877–1967) and many others paved the way for Harkness's address. Southard, an author and licensed lay pastor from Kansas, offered an epoch-making resolution from the floor of the 1920 MEC General Conference:

> Whereas, Today the principle of equality of opportunity for women is being recognized in all fields of activity; and
>
> Whereas, This General Conference has gone on record as urging political equality for women by requesting the Delaware house of representatives to sign the Susan B. Anthony amendment; therefore be it
>
> Resolved, The General Conference approve ecclesiastical equality for women, that it remove all restrictions and limitations upon women in the service of the church, and that it instruct the proper committee to make any changes in the Discipline necessary to accomplish this end.[49]

Pastor Southard followed her resolution with an exegetically nuanced speech describing how the church's mistaken interpretation of Bible passages (like 1 Cor 14:34–35) had been used to shamefully silence the voices of talented Methodist women like Frances Willard and Anna Shaw, women who had been authentically called by God to preach the gospel.[50] After significant debate, the resolution was referred to the "Committee on the Itineracy," and after four days of deliberation the Committee recommended that women be accepted into Methodist ministry under the category of "local pastors" (a lay position), while a study commission was formed to bring the issue of ordination forward at the 1924 MEC General Conference.

At the 1924 MEC General Conference, Dr. Georgia Harkness addressed the same governing body that had refused to hear the voice of the

47. Keller, *Georgia Harkness*, 114.

48. Keller, *Georgia Harkness* 58.

49. Irons, "From Kansas to the World," 35–36.

50. Nickell, *We Shall Not Be Moved*, 66–69.

MEC's female director of the Women's Home Missions Society only four-teen years before.[51] Harkness's arguments regarding the prejudicial treat-ment of women were unassailable because they were based in her own lived experiences:

> A few remarkably gifted women . . . have been able to make a place for themselves in the ministry, but there the Church which would not choose a mediocre man in preference to a superior woman is one among a thousand.
>
> I do not maintain that this prejudice can be attributed ex-clusively to the ministers themselves, for most of them are more broad-minded than their congregations. There is . . . a deep seated relic of medievalism in the attitude of the Church at large which the clergy has not done all it might to eradicate. Such is the shortage of ministers that in many denominations almost any man of good moral character and religious convictions can get a pulpit. But when men are permitted to preach whose edu-cation does not extend beyond the eighth grade, and women college trained and sometimes theologically trained are denied the privilege, something is wrong.[52]

After heated debate, the General Conference narrowly voted to allow women to be ordained as local pastors and deacons but could not agree to grant women status of full clergy members of an annual conference. The motion blocking full clergy status for women argued that it would cause the MEC "peculiar and embarrassing difficulties" of having to guarantee women a pastoral appointment.[53] By the spring of 1927, eighty-one women had been ordained as deacons in the MEC, and were moving into Elder's Orders. Among these were Georgia Harkness herself, she received Elder's Orders in 1939.[54] These women were ordained, but since they were denied full membership in the Annual Conferences, they could not be appointed to a ministry. Meanwhile, the reunion of the MEC North and South with the MPC in 1939 came at the cost of forcing the MPC tradition to drop its policy of full female participation through ordination.

The Women's Division of the MEC brought petitions for full clergy status and function for women to the Methodist General Conferences of 1944, 1948, 1952, and another 2,000 petitions with a similar aim came to the 1956 MEC General Conference. But their struggle for equality and reform

---

51. Richey et al., *Methodist Experience*, I:346–48.

52. Richey et al., *Methodist Experience*, II:511–12.

53. Nickell, *We Shall Not Be Moved*, 66–70.

54. Richey et al., *Methodist Experience*, I:348.

was, as Jane Nickell described it, "A Process Still Controlled By Men."[55] A compromise was suggested that would allow single and widowed women to receive full clergy status, but not married ones; obviously, "the proper place" of a married woman was still at home. The compromise motion failed, and after a strong debate a motion was made from the floor that "women are included in all the provisions referring to ministers" in the MEC *Discipline*; the motion passed with a show of hands. Harkness remarked, "I think I have seen a miracle twice this week."[56] Not only had a woman preached before the MEC General Conference, but all Methodist women were given the opportunity to aspire to full clergy status. It was, however, seventy-six years too late for Ms. Shaw and Oliver and so many others. Despite the many difficulties some women faced in their pastoral appointments, the gradual social shift toward the full equality of women and men moderated the church's prejudice over time.

The final step toward full inclusion was symbolized by the election of Marjorie Swank Matthews (1918–86), as bishop in the United Methodist Church in 1980. This event represented the apex of the trajectory that began so many years earlier and was maintained in the long struggle for the ordination of women. In Bishop Marjorie Matthews a woman not only reached the highest office in the church, but she was also in a position to approve and ordain other women. Bishop Matthews considered her election to be a new beginning, and not a culmination:

Artist unknown, *Bishop Marjorie*, **from the General Commission on Archives and History of the United Methodist Church, Madison, New Jersey, used with permission.**

> I do not . . . regard my election as the culmination of the feminist movement within the United Methodist Church. I still believe that recognition and acceptance of women clergy and the leadership of women in the entire church is an idea whose time was long overdue. There is a big job ahead for clergy persons everywhere, and a challenge to the church to remain faithful to the teachings of our Lord, Jesus Christ. I am committed to that challenge and struggle.[57]

55. Nickell, *We Shall Not Be Moved*, 77–83.

56. Richey et al., *Methodist Experience*, I:402–3.

57. "Bishop Marjorie Matthews," an unpublished document, Colgate Rochester Crozer Divinity School Archives, Rochester, NY.

Methodist women used a variety of approaches and strategies as they moved toward greater opportunities for service and more equality. Initially, they stretched and redefined the cultural limitations they faced and turned private virtues into public vocations. They also injected new ideas into the old models, like the many women who exercised their "extraordinary call" to preach so successfully that the ordinary rules against them doing so had to be laid aside. There were also many women who turned new parachurch works, like the revivals of the Second Great Awakening, into new spirit-directed spaces where the old prohibitions did not apply. When they faced dead ends in male-dominated church agencies women raised their own funds and created their own agencies, like the Methodist Female Home Missions Society. When their way forward to significant service was blocked by prejudice and patriarchal barriers, Methodist women sometimes stepped outside of the church to do the same service through benevolent societies like the WCTU. But ultimately full ordination and institutional inclusion came only by working tirelessly so that over time both attitudes and opportunities changed. For some women, this meant leaving one church in order to serve a more willing one; for others, it meant committing themselves to an ongoing struggle for full equality.

FOR FURTHER CONSIDERATION:

1. The exclusion of women from leadership roles in Methodism was rooted in a particular way of reading the Bible, the weight of tradition, patriarchal social norms, and prejudice. Which of these was the most difficult to overcome?

2. What lessons can you learn by observing women's journey from having "extraordinary" opportunity to preach toward official recognition and full equality in the church?

3. Over the centuries Methodist women gradually climbed a ladder from domestic leadership and unofficial roles to public leadership and ordination. What are the life lessons you draw from this story?

4. Methodist women have used a variety of strategies as they moved toward greater opportunities for service and greater equality. What were they? What is the importance of this?

5. Women continue to face a "stained-glass ceiling" in that their leadership is often marginalized or restricted in tacit ways. Why is that? What can you do?

CHAPTER 16

"Eleven O'Clock on Sunday Morning"

Controversy over Racism and Segregation in America

EARLY METHODIST CLASS ROLLS from New York and Philadelphia evidence the inclusion of African American people in predominantly white, lay-led American Methodism. Sometimes the black participants were servants of other class members, which could have been a significant barrier to egalitarianism, but positive relationships were formed nonetheless. Interracial friendships also were formed in the home meetings conducted by rural itinerants. As John Ellis opined: "The Methodist anti-slavery politics was sharpened by cottage religion. Their intimate and ecstatic meetings could temporarily bridge the racial divide. For example, William Colbert described one service in which two white Maryland men shouted and danced with worshipping blacks, 'not ashamed' to join them in praising God."[1] Perhaps the greatest gift these early face-to-face relationships gave early American Methodism was empathy, as Ellis noted: "Many itinerants empathized with their black converts. . . . Nineteen-year-old John Kohler typified this empathy when he noted in 1789 that he had met several Virginia slaves living in squalor who were his grandfather's age. He then unleased righteous fury toward the 'very rich' whites in his class who ignored those blacks 'reduced so low it absolutely is a scandal.'"[2] But these early interracial acquaintances were not potent enough to overcome the propensity of Americans' original sin when it came to "the amalgamation of the races."[3]

1. Ellis, "Pragmatic Radicals," 21–22.
2. Ellis, "Pragmatic Radicals," 21.
3. Ellis, "Pragmatic Radicals," 21.

Several prominent early Methodist preachers, including Bishops Francis Asbury, Thomas Coke, Freeborn Garrettson, and Jesse Lee, were ardent abolitionists who faced mob violence for their views. When Garrettson converted to Methodism in 1775, abolitionist sentiments came along with his newfound faith in Christ: "I shall always have an aversion to the practice of holding our fellow-creatures in abject slavery. It was the blessed God that taught me the rights of man."[4] Freeborn felt compelled to liberate his own slaves, and evangelized black audiences, both slave and free, with great regularity.

Asbury and Garrettson worked closely with two extraordinary African American preachers, Harry Hosier (1750–1806) and Richard Allen (1760–1831). Early Methodism was, as Ian B. Straker pointed out, "Black, and White and Gray all over." The "gray" area had to do with the ambiguity and ambivalence that even racially sensitive Methodists felt between the opposition of slavery and actually accepting people of African descent as their equals. Straker noted, "The mixed and even conflicting views that African and white Methodists held of each other allowed for warm and even friendly and supportive relationships to exist despite the nonegalitarian views of African progress and civil rights held by Garrettson and others."[5] When it came to acknowledging the contributions of those black men, either in their publications or by granting them clergy standing in the MEC, as Richey et al. reported, "Methodists had a hard time 'recognizing' Black leadership, in the sense of writing it out of the record and of refusing to legitimate Black leaders on the record with formal credentials. It would be another decade, not till 1800, that the MEC would permit African Americans even the status of local deacon."[6]

Harry Hosier, often called "Black Harry," was the first prominent African American preacher of the early decades of American Methodism. On June 28, 1780, Harry Hosier came to the attention of Bishop Francis Asbury, as Asbury planned a preaching tour of the mid-south. "I have thought if I had two horses," Asbury wrote, "and Harry (a colored man) to go with and drive one, and meet the black people, and to spend about six months in Virginia and the Carolinas, it would be attended with a blessing."[7] Hosier faced great hostility while ministering in the American South, but nowhere was he immune from it; in Boston, for example, Freeborn Garrettson recalled, "when Harry gave an exhortation several rude people behaved

4. Bangs, *Life of the Rev. Freeborn Garrettson*, 39–40.

5. Straker, "Black and White and Gray," 27.

6. Richey et al., *Methodist Experience*, I:60.

7. Clark, *Journal and Letters of Francis Asbury*, I:362.

uncivilly."[8] The hostility and threats of violence that Asbury's abolitionist sermons and Hosier's ministry elicited may have contributed to Harry's ambiguous vocational identity; he was often referred to as Asbury's "servant" or "driver," instead of being described as a "preacher." It is likely there were occasions when working within conventional racial social roles opened doors that may have been otherwise closed, and forestalled violence. But Warren Thomas Smith describing Harry's relationship with his white ministerial colleagues as "affable paternalism" rings true.[9] While white Methodism's appreciation for Harry Hosier as a man and preacher deepened and grew as they learned to think of him as a talented evangelist, Smith's warning is helpful: "We must be careful not to paint an unreal picture. Elevated though he may have been, Hosier never seems to have stood on exactly the same footing with the others."[10]

Artist unknown, *Harry Hosier*, from the General Commission of Archives and History of the United Methodist Church, Madison, New Jersey, used with permission.

Over the course of nearly thirty years of active ministry Harry Hosier "traveled" with many of the luminaries of American Methodism. The term that most often appears in the historical record describing his preaching is "eloquent," and in an America textured by myths of black inferiority, a capable Methodist preacher of African descent was also a novelty that drew large, mixed audiences. Hosier's popularity went well beyond novelty, however, as Henry Boehm reported: "Crowds flocked to hear him, not only because he was a colored man, but because he was eloquent. Mr. Asbury wished him to travel with him for the benefit of the colored people."[11] There was a clear connection between Methodism's use of prominent black preachers, like Harry Hosier and Richard Allen, and the movement's exponential growth and popularity among African Americans. The demographics bear this out: African American participation in the MEC stood at 11,682 black members in 1790 (the first year for which church-wide demographics are available), and culminated at 166,885 on the eve of

8. Bangs, *Life of the Rev. Freeborn Garrettson*, 190.
9. Smith, *Harry Hosier*, 44.
10. Smith, *Harry Hosier*, 44.
11. Boehm, *Reminiscences*, 90.

the American Civil War in 1858; in its first sixty years Methodist evangelism made significant inroads into the African American community.[12]

Harry Hosier's official status with the MEC was that of "an exhorter," that is—one who spoke after the main sermon to augment and bring home the main points of the previous message. The difference between "preaching" and "exhorting" was sometimes as confusing then as it sounds now, and quite a lot of what Harry Hosier actually did was preaching from a text. But "exhorters" were not paid and "traveling preachers" were, so the difference in terminology was significant. Given the herculean service that Harry gave the MEC for more than twenty years, one wonders why he was not ordained deacon along with Richard Allen when the quantity and quality of his work indicated he deserved it. Hosier was granted a local license to preach by St. George's MEC in Philadelphia, with which he served an African society there (1794), and then African Zoar Church (1796).[13] By the turn of the century, Harry disappeared from the ministries in Philadelphia and New York, and there is uncertainty about his end. It does seem, however, there was disaffection between him and the Methodists. As Dr. Harry V. Richardson reported:

> The main reason these men [Hosier, Richard Allen, and others] left the Methodist Church was the reluctance of that body to accept them fully into its ministry. The Church did not recognize their preaching and organizing abilities, especially in the work with blacks, and used them as exhorters and local preachers, the lowest orders in the Methodist hierarchy. But despite repeated appeals over a long time, the Church would not ordain them as deacons, the middle rank, and certainly not as elders, the highest rank.[14]

Richard Allen (1760–1831) was born into slavery (Philadelphia), and spent his youth working on Stokley Sturgis's plantation in Delaware, where he learned several trades and taught himself to read and write. He was converted under the preaching of a Methodist evangelist (Garrettson?), and was able to buy his freedom through his craftsmanship. Relocating to the Philadelphia area, Allen began to testify and preach before small groups of Christians. When he became affiliated with the Methodists, Richard Allen itinerated in eastern Pennsylvania where he "traveled the Hartford Circuit with Mr. Porters, who traveled that circuit."[15] After attending the 1784 Gen-

---

12. Finke and Stark, *Churching of America*, 100.

13. Shockley, "Methodist Episcopal Church," 52.

14. Richardson, "Early Black Methodist Preachers," 3.

15. Allen, *Life Experiences*, 11.

eral Conference where the Methodist preachers "were said to be entitled to the gown," Allen began to harbor doubts about the Methodist movement's transition into the Methodist Episcopal Church: "I have thought religion has been declining in the church ever since," he wrote.[16]

After itinerating with Rev. Richard Whatcoat on the Baltimore circuit of the MEC, in the autumn of 1785, Richard Allen returned to Philadelphia, where he began working as an assistant at St. George's Church, in February 1786. Soon he was preaching as often as "four to five times a day," and conducting prayer meetings. As his predominately black Methodist society grew to more than forty-two members, Richard Allen saw the need for a separate Black Methodist church, but this idea ran afoul of the white establishment:

Artist unknown, *Rev'd Richard Allen, Bishop of the First African Methodist Episcopal Church of the US*, **from the New York Public Library Digital Commons, the Miriam and Ira D. Wallach Division of Art, Prints, and Photographs, Print Collection, public domain.**

> Mr. W[hatcoat]—was much opposed to an African church, and used very degrading and insulting language to us, to try and prevent us from going on. We all belonged to St. George's Church—Rev. Absalom Jones, William White, and Dorus Ginnings. We felt ourselves much cramped; but my dear Lord was with us, and we believed, if it was his will, the work would go on, and that we would be able to succeed in building the house of the Lord.[17]

The rapidly growing constituency of African Americans at St. George's was initially received with joy but soon became a source of irritation to some white parishioners. Tensions increased as Allen, Absalom Jones, and others led classes and began "building a black niche within St. George's," as Richard A. Newman described it.[18] The black preachers also conducted "exhortation meetings" off-site, which were "emotional mini-revivals reminiscent of circuit preaching."[19] At some point the blacks attending St. George's MEC were relegated to the "gallery" (or balcony), where they often took seats near

16. Allen, *Life Experiences*, 11–12.

17. Allen, *Life Experiences*, 13–14.

18. Newman, *Freedom's Prophet*, 59.

19. Newman, *Freedom's Prophet*, 59.

the front. One day, while the whole congregation knelt in prayer, two St. George's trustees took hold of Rev. Jones and tried to haul him to his feet, so that he could be relocated to the rear. Richard Allen recalled,

> Mr. Jones said, "Wait until the prayer is over, and I will get up and trouble you no more." . . . By this time the prayer was over, and we all went out of the church in a body, and they were no more plagued with us in the church. This raised a great excitement and inquiry among the citizens, in so much that I believe they were ashamed of their conduct. But my dear Lord was with us, and we were filled with fresh vigor to get a house erected to worship God in.[20]

Richard Allen's earliest account of the "walk out" seems to set the event in year 1787,[21] but recent research suggests a date in 1792–93 may be more likely.[22] The debate about the date of the black "walk out" of St. George's MEC is not merely a dispute about historical facts it also has bearing on the interpretation the event receives. Did the people of African descent leave, or were they forced out? Likely it's a bit of both; the black Methodists were being forced out of their seats at St. George's MEC. Their response to that

William L. Breton, *Bethel African Methodist Episcopal Church, Philadaelphia, Founded in 1794 by the Revd. Richard Allen, Bishop of the first African Methodist Episcopal Church in the United States, rebuilt in 1805,* **drawn on stone, Philadelphia, PA, 1829. From the Digital Collection of the Library Company of Philadelphia.**

situation was an act of protest, like that of Ms. Rosa Parks, who refused to relinquish her seat in the front of the Birmingham bus in 1955.

In July of 1794, Richard Allen and other black Methodists established a separate church and built a small-frame structure, which was blessed by Bishop Francis Asbury. Asbury's journal reported, "Sunday 29, I preached at the new African church. Our colored brethren are to be governed by the doctrine and discipline of the Methodists."[23] But Allen recalled, "Our warfare and

---

20. Allen, *Life Experiences*, 14.

21. Allen, *Life Experiences*, 14.

22. Newman, *Freedom's Prophet*, 65–66.

23. Clark, *Journal and Letters of Francis Asbury*, II:19.

troubles now began afresh," because the MEC Conference insisted upon taking ownership of their building—as was the case with all other Methodist churches. Allen and his colleagues "told him [Asbury] they *might* deny us their name, but they could *not* deny us a seat in heaven."[24] After another series of strained conversations, and a congregational vote by the African American congregation at Bethel MEC, they unanimously decided to incorporate as a separate church outside of the institutional control of the MEC. By 1795, "mother" Bethel Church was a community numbering 121 people. Under Richard Allen's leadership, it blossomed to 457 by 1803, and 1,272 in 1813.[25] In 1799, Bishop Asbury ordained Richard Allen as deacon, and then again as elder (1816). And although struggles with the MEC over jurisdiction and oversight continued, Rev. Allen's commitment to Methodism never wavered. As he explained to Bishop Francis Asbury: "Our one design is to secure to ourselves our rights and privileges, to regulate our affairs, temporal and spiritual, the same as white people, and to guard against any opposition which might possibly arise from the improper prejudices or administration of any individual having the exercise of discipline over us."[26]

In 1816, Bethel Church aligned herself with African American congregations in Baltimore, Wilmington, Delaware, Salem, New Jersey, and Attleboro, Pennsylvania to form the African Methodist Episcopal (AME), and Rev. Richard Allen was elected as the AME's first bishop. The AME Church retained the theological heritage and organizational structure of the MEC, but sought independence from an institution that had lost the trust and respect of the members of their community. The establishment of the African Methodist Episcopal Church Zion under the leadership of James Varick (1750?–1827), out of a black remnant of John's Street MEC in New York City, followed a similar pattern in 1820, while the Colored Methodist Episcopal Church (CMEC) was organized by mutual consent of the white and black constituencies of the MEC South, in the post-Civil War

Thomas Coke Ruckle, *The Ordination of Bishop Francis Asbury by Bishop Thomas Coke* **(1882), an engraving by A. Glichrist Campbell from the original painting. Located at the Drew University Methodist Collection, Madison, NJ, public domain. A cropped close-up of Harry Hosier standing in the background.**

24. Allen, *Life Experiences*, 20. Emphasis added.

25. Andrews, *Methodists and Revolutionary America,* 149–50.

26. Clark, *Journal and Letters of Francis Asbury,* III:367.

segregationist climate of 1870. While taking different routes, the AMEC, the AMEC Zion, and the CMEC each navigated their way through the challenges of a culture shaped by white supremacy and racial segregation.

The famous painting *The Ordination of Bishop Asbury*, by Thomas Coke Ruckle (1882), depicts very well the MEC's understanding of the place of Harry Hosier and Richard Allen in the church. If you look very carefully, just past the pulpit that dominates the left side of the portrait, and down and to the right, you can catch a glimpse of Harry Hosier, standing at the far back edge of the throng. We look in vain, however, for Richard Allen who was also present at the event; Allen's ecclesial exclusion was mirrored by the painting. Taken together, the exemplary lives of Harry Hosier and Richard Allen seemed to offer people of African descent, within the MEC, two different two models of dealing with racism in America. "The coachman or the proprietor" was how the unnamed editor of Philadelphia's black newspaper, *The Christian Recorder*, described them:

> Hosier traveled with Bishop Asbury as a coachman, preaching to the colored people, but afterwards becoming popular with the white people as a preacher. He ended his days in the M.E.C., bearing in that Church all the inconsistencies and ungodly prejudice that that must have characterized American Christianity among Caucasians in his day as they do in our times, a servant in a servant's place. . . . Richard Allen lead[s] in laying the foundation of self-assertiveness by the colored people in religious matters, building churches, incorporating societies, organizing a denomination, preparing the race for the enjoyment of general freedom. . . . By means of which course has the colored man made the better, more serviceable and more widely recognized manhood; the coachman's or the proprietor's?[27]

The approach taken by Harry Hosier allowed him to work within white-dominated culture and survive, and perhaps to sometimes thrive with the tacit hope that he was changing minds and lives one person at a time. The more confrontational road taken by Richard Allen led to more dignity and self-determination but ultimately also to separation and segregation. Black Methodists have navigated their path through life in America by embracing both aspects of this complicated dichotomy.

Methodist preacher and historian Jesse Lee remembered that the Christmas Conference of 1784 ruled, "Every member in our Society who has slaves, in those states where the laws will admit of freeing them, shall, after notice given him by the preacher, within twelve months . . . legally

27. Lee, "Harry Hosier."

execute and record an instrument, whereby he set free every slave in his possession."[28] The 1784 antislavery rules carried the sanction of excommunication and expulsion; the buying and selling of slaves, "unless on purpose to free them," was grounds for expulsion.[29] The 1784 prohibitions reflected the tacit belief, one that was shared by Asbury and Garrettson, that slavery would die a gradual death in the newly freed America. In their assumption about the success of gradualism, Methodist rules allowed a dangerous caveat: "in those states where the laws will admit of freeing them."[30] This caveat was a disaster for the abolitionists since it short-circuited any push for political redress, gave Methodists in slave-holding states moral "cover" since they were only "obeying the laws" while keeping slaves, and it allowed more and more states to pass proslavery legislation.

The 1785 Annual Conference added a stronger-sounding statement: "We do hold in the deepest abhorrence the practice of slavery and shall not cease to seek its destruction, by all *wise and prudent* means."[31] While one could debate whether a particular "means" was "wise and prudent," a different debate was going on behind the scenes; one which Richey et al. saw evidenced in two letters Francis Asbury wrote to Freeborn Garrettson. In 1785, the bishop stated, "With respect to slavery, I am clear, and always was, that if every Preacher would do his duty we should not need to make any Minutes, use no force, but only loving and argumentative persuasion." A second letter hinted at a connection in Bishop Asbury's thinking between a gradualist approach toward abolition and the rising costs of financing the movement on the one hand and the increasing role played by affluent donors: "Do not be so anxious about building houses," Asbury wrote. "We groan under a heavy debt in [New] York, Philadelphia and Baltimore and it weakens the hands of the poor among us and strengthens the hand of the few rich to oppose our strictness and discipline."[32] The predominantly white MEC was beginning to be riven by controversy caused by racism at the very same time it faced a financial crisis that created undue influence for wealthy Methodists, and in the South wealthy Methodists were invariably plantation-owing slaveholders. Rev. Jessie Lee, who was present at each of the early MEC Conferences, chronicled the deterioration of "the rules" prohibiting slavery: "These rules were short lived, and were offensive to most of

28. Lee, *Short History*, 97.

29. Lee, *Short History*, 97.

30. Lee, *Short History*, 97.

31. Scott, *Appeal*, 11. Emphasis added.

32. Richey et al., *Methodist Experience*, 59. They cited these letters from unpublished manuscripts.

our southern friends; and were so much opposed by many of our private members, local preachers, and some of the traveling preachers, that the execution of them was suspended at the conference held in June following, about six months after they were formed; and they were never afterwards carried into full force."[33]

Orange Scott (1800–47) published *Appeal to the Methodist Episcopal Church,* which detailed the erosion of the MEC's abolitionism and described it as "The Retrograde March of the

scribed it as "The Retrograde March of the Church." In his chapter by that same title, Rev. Scott supplied documentary evidence of "the downhill course of the Methodist Episcopal Church on the subject of slavery for the *last sixty* years."[34] He pointed out that not only had the univocal language against slavery disappeared from MEC's *Book of Discipline,* even the moderate statement published in 1801 that the MEC "more than ever convinced of the great evil of slavery" was "acknowledged on all hands to be *dead letter*" because financial and political issues made it unenforceable.[35]

Artist unknown, *Orange Scott (1800–1847),* **in Lucius Matlack,** *The Life of Orange Scott,* **2 vols. (New York: Wesleyan Book Room, 1847), from Association of Religion Data Archives, public domain.**

The 1836 MEC General Conference was more concerned about the divisive abolitionist fervor evidenced by some of its ministers than the slaveholding practices of others. Dominated by fear of potential schism, the Conference passed a gag order against the abolitionist agitators: "[It is] resolved, by the delegates of the annual conferences, in the General Conference assembled, that they are decidedly opposed to modern abolitionism, and wholly disclaim any right, wish, or intention to interfere in the civil and political relationship between master and slave, as it exists in the slaveholding states of this union." The resolution attacking "modern abolitionism" passed by a stunningly one-sided vote of 120–14.[36] By 1838, Rev. Scott predicted that the MEC would have to decide between having "a Slave-Holding Bishop—or a Division of the Church."[37] In this politically charged climate, Nathan Bangs (1778–1862), the voice of "establishment

---

33. Lee, *Short History,* 97–98.

34. Scott, *Appeal,* 12. Emphasis original.

35. Scott, *Appeal,* 12.

36. Scott, *Appeal,* 14.

37. Scott, *Appeal,* 14.

Methodism," added an editorial caution to the views of Freeborn Garrettson when he republished the abolitionist's biography in 1838: "In the present state of things in the southern states it seems unavailable to contend for emancipation."[38]

How can one account for this stunning reversal of MEC opinion and the "General Rules?" Don Matthews summarized the situation succinctly: "The Methodist clergy would have to make the choice between purity and popularity."[39] It could also be argued that changing times required changing attitudes. The social climate of America was changing dramatically; Christian social radicalism—which had been a part of Methodism DNA from the outset—was no longer fashionable and had become loathsome for some. The establishment of the African Colonialization Society in 1817 offered what looked like a compromise solution to the problem of America's original sin. For whites, in particular, the program's connection to the "Great Commission" of Christianity and the potential "uplift" for African American people provided moral cover for their racist and segregationist attitudes about sending them "home" to Africa. And it is also difficult to discern how deeply the "slave revolts" led by Denmark Vesey (1822) and Nat Turner

E. Mackensie, Rev. *Nathan Bangs, D.D.*, **an engraving made from a portrait by John Paradise (1783–1833), in Nathan Bangs,** *The History of the Methodist Episcopal Church*, **2 vols. (New York: The Methodist Book Concern, 1838).**

(1831) contributed to negative attitudes about a biracial vision for America and gave new potency to fears harbored by southern slaveholders and other whites.

The MEC showdown over the slavery question, which Orange Scott had anticipated when he wrote in 1838, came to pass in 1844. But Scott and many of his abolitionist colleagues were already gone by then, having walked out of the MEC in 1842–43 to form the Wesleyan Methodist Church. They were soon followed by Rev. B. T. Roberts and the "Free Methodists" in 1860. At the 1844 General Conference, Rev. James Osgood Andrews (1794–1871), a slaveholding MEC bishop from Georgia, became the lightning rod for the Methodist debate over slavery. When Bishop Andrews refused to emancipate his slaves, the General Conference passed a resolution requiring him to "desist" from exercising the office of bishop as

38. Bangs, *Life of the Rev. Freeborn Garrettson*, 60.
39. Mathews, *Methodism and Slavery*, 18.

long as he owned slaves. When the resolution prohibiting Andrews passed 110–69 strictly along North-South regional lines it was clear that the MEC was headed toward the schism. Schism was not long in coming; the next spring, the Southern Annual Conferences of the MEC met in Louisville to establish anew the Methodist Episcopal Church South.

The old saying, "time heals all wounds," may be true—but the word "slowly" needs to be added. The MEC North and South had begun commissions probing for ways to cooperate with each other at the end of the nineteenth century, and by 1916 the quest for "cooperation" became one for "reunion" when an interdenominational, multiracial "Joint Commission on Unification" was established. It is important to juxtapose the MEC plan for reunion with the vast popularity of *Birth of a Nation* (1915), a feature film celebrating white supremacy and the "lost cause" ideology of the New South by D. W. Griffith with the MEC reunion conversations.[40] Because of its glorification of the Klu Klux Klan and white supremacy, John Hope Franklin credited it with fueling the rebirth of the KKK.[41] In this racially charged social climate the Methodist reunion talks of 1916 went nowhere.

The question of Methodist reunion laid dormant until 1929 when the Methodist Protestant Church opted to join the conversation and this was the impetus for the unification process once again. Each of the three partners appointed their own study commissions and these led up to join meetings, beginning in 1934. A plan of union was hammered out, which bore some similarity to the one that failed in 1916, at least on the matter of race and race relations. The new MEC talked about greater racial harmony, but it planned for racial segregation by creating the "Central Jurisdiction" (CJ) as an organizational and governance entity for black Methodist churches. The CJ did *not* stop white and black Methodists from worshiping and working together, but it certainly did not encourage it either. It meant, in fact, that they would not *have* to work and worship together very often. Jane Ellen Nickell rightly termed the 1936 General Conference as "a union defined by racial division."[42]

The racial situation at the Methodist reunion was so complex and emotionally charged that historical commentators cannot *even* agree whether or not the eleven African American delegates at the planning meetings voted *for* the plan of union, that included the CJ, or not.[43] But from the floor of the

40. Davis, "Birth of a Nation," 23–44.

41. Franklin, "Birth of a Nation," 430–31.

42. Nickell, *We Shall Not Be Moved*, 39–45.

43. Sledge, "Step Back," 10–22; see esp. the "Historiography" subsection for a survey of the literature.

May 5, 1936 General Conference session of the MEC, Rev. David D. Jones, a black clergy delegate from North Carolina, spoke on behalf of thirty-three African American delegates to "protest in a mild, but manly way against this Plan of Unification":

> Everyone knows the Plan is segregation, and segregation in the ugliest way, because it is couched in such pious terms. . . . This Plan turns its back on the historic attitude of the Methodist Episcopal Church. All through the years we have had interracial fellowship. Some people are good enough to say that the Negros have made more progress than any other race so situated. I say to you if we have made progress it has been in a measure due to the kind of fellowship and the kind of leadership we have had. Do you ask us today to turn our backs on . . . people who have come and given their lives to us? We cannot do it. In conclusion, you may adopt this plan. We are powerless to prevent it, absolutely powerless. All we can do is appeal to time.[44]

Major Jones described the black Methodist's response to the Plan of Union as "Passive Resistance," a plan which, in the words of Dr. James P. Brawley, was "a stigma too humiliating to accept."[45] The terse headline from *The Crisis*, an official publication of the NAACP (June 1936) gave voice to the betrayal felt by many African Americans when it described the MEC Plan of Union as "Jim Crow for Jesus."[46]

Many of the delegates, particularly white delegates, argued that gradual change was necessary because in the current situation the "perfect" solution of an integrated church was unattainable, and it could, in fact, become the unconscious enemy of a "good" solution. Rev. Lynn Harold Hough, for example, viewed the CJ as a practicable step in the right direction, doing something instead of nothing; one step that could be followed by other steps: "when we ask [for] what in a particular situation we cannot have; instead of being content to take a step, doing that century after century the really on-going movement of the Kingdom of God has been made practically impossible."[47] Once again, gradualism led to regressive Methodist policies on race. Looking back at the establishment of the CJ, Dr. William McClain concluded: "in setting up the Central Jurisdiction, the Methodist Church capitulated to the counter currents of American racist proclivities and yielded to the prevailing morality of the society. Its ethic became those

44. Richey et al., *Methodist Experience*, II:549.
45. Jones, "Central Jurisdiction," 195.
46. Carter, "Negro and Methodist Union," 60.
47. Richey et al., *Methodist Experience*, II:548.

temporal pragmatic considerations of the world rather than the eternal claims of justice which its prophetic Lord had declared."[48]

Arguments for gradual change continued for another three decades, offered often by well-intentioned whites who lacked the will or insight to see how deeply damaging complicity with evil is for everyone involved. Not only did the CJ explicitly devalue African Americans, it implicitly deprived Euro-Americans (and others) of concrete opportunities to debunk demonic cultural myths—like black inferiority and white supremacy—through meaningful interracial relationships. Thirty years later, Dr. Martin Luther King still heard so many gradualist arguments coming from "white support-ers" that he titled his first chronicle of the struggle for civil justice, *Why We Can't Wait*.[49] Rev. King's indictment of "white moderate" Christians in his *Letter from a Birmingham Jail* could have easily been directed to the MEC:

> Over the past few years I have been gravely disappointed with the white moderate. I have almost reached the regrettable conclusion that the Negro's great stumbling block in his stride toward freedom is . . . the white moderate, who is more devoted to "order" than to justice; who prefers a negative peace which is the absence of tension to a positive peace which is the presence of justice; who constantly says: "I agree with you in the goal you seek, but I cannot agree with your methods of direct action"; who paternalistically believes he can set the timetable for an-other man's freedom.[50]

It was in the context of the gradually changing racial climate of the 1960s that the MEC and the Evangelical United Brethren Churches began conversations about unification that Dr. King's observation, first made in an interview on *Meet the Press*, encapsulated the magnitude of challenge that lay ahead. "I think it is one of the tragedies of our nation, one of the shame-ful tragedies, that eleven o'clock on Sunday morning is one of the most seg-regated hours, if not the most segregated hour, in Christian America," King observed. "I definitely think the Christian church should be integrated, and any church that stands against integration and that has a segregated body is standing against the spirit and the teachings of Jesus Christ, and it fails to be a true witness. But this is *something* that the church will have to do itself."[51] That "something" began in 1963, when a group representing the Evangelical United Brethren pastors and theologians raised the importance

48. McClain, *Black People*, 85.

49. King, *Why We Can't Wait*.

50. West, *Radical King*, 135.

51. King, "Interview." Emphasis added.

of dissolving the MEC Central Jurisdiction as they began conversations that led to union with the MEC.

From clergy assignments to office staff and publicity materials, racial inclusion and institutional desegregation of the MEC was a vital aspect of the unification plan that was agreed upon and implemented when the United Methodist Church was born in 1968. Speaking on behalf of the newly formed Black Methodists for Church Renewal, James M. Lawson reported:

> The Methodist Church has never listened to responsible Negro leadership. In 1939 Negro Methodists rejected segregation. Yet union dictated the creation of the Central Jurisdiction. From that time on Negroes agitated for the integrated church. Only Central Jurisdiction leaders made an effort to study, discuss, and define "The Inclusive Church" and how racism could be ended at all levels of the church. Their counsel and advice were summarily refused. Since 1964 mergers in Methodism have not been grounded in Christian encounter, grass-root faith, and programming or courageous leadership. Today, most white Methodists still suspect that the Gospel of Jesus Christ and racial myths are consonant.[52]

The year 1972 was set as the target date for the desegregation of all UMC institutions, programs, facilities, and churches. To implement that process, the UMC "General Commission on Religion and Race" was established (1968), in order to "address the turbulent and exciting unrest, disease, hope, and new possibilities unleashed as legalized racial segregation and separation were being dismantled in church and society."[53]

One of the places where change has been implemented was in the episcopate, through the election of black leaders for the new church. This was illustrated in the election of Rev. Roy C. Nicholas (who ordained me in Pittsburgh), as the first black bishop of the new UMC in 1968. With biracial leadership came significant cross-cultural pastoral appointments, which brought challenges to both pastors and congregations as the UMC struggled to work out its commitment to racial inclusion in real terms. Denominational leaders were sometimes criticized for attempting "social engineering through

Artist unknown, *Bishop Roy C. Nicholas*, **from the General Commission on Archives and History, Madison, New Jersey, with permission.**

52. Richey et al., *Methodist Experience*, II:613.

53. Medley, "Racism Influences Methodist History."

the appointment system."[54] And yet, Martin Luther King's observation about 11 a.m. on Sunday morning rings nearly as true today as it did sixty years ago. But perhaps the UMC can say with Rev. King, "that my church is not a segregating church. It's segregated but *not* segregating."[55]

In a recent article, Dr. William McClain, explored the question raised by the subtitle of his book *Black People in the Methodist Church: Whither Thou Goest?*[56] Black people in the UMC demon-

strated "a fierce fidelity" by staying with the church in greater numbers than their white sisters and brothers, McClain pointed out. After he explored the reasons *why* black people were attracted to Methodism in the first place, and *why* they stayed, he also considered why black people should continue to participate in the Methodist Church, despite its past failures. Dr. McClain pointed to several aspects: 1) their shared hope for a better future, based in God's grace; 2) the continuation of what Wesley called "Scriptural Christianity"—that is, a willingness to major in life-giving core Christian beliefs; 3) their desire

Mike DuBois, UMC News, *Dr. William Bobby McClain,* **used with permission.**

"to affirm and live out a belief in the gospel they heard"; 4) to claim their own heritage; 5) African Methodists can be "a missional presence" in their own church; 6) and they can "be the primordial conscience of Methodism"—in order to help Methodists and all Christians live up to the inclusive gospel they affirm.[57]

The story of race relations in Methodism is, as Ian Straker described it, "Black, and White and Gray All Over."[58] There were shining moments of white inclusion and empowerment of people of African descent. Despite the powerful presence and contribution of exemplary black Methodists like Harry Hosier, Richard Allen, James Varick, Jarena Lee, Amanda Berry Smith, and so many others throughout the history of the Methodist Church, however, with respect to black people Methodist history too often reads like a long chronicle of missed opportunities. What if the MEC had retained and enforced its prohibition of slavery? What if the 1936 MEC framers of the Plan of Union had heard and heeded the voices of the black Methodist

54. King, "Interview."

55. King, "Interview."

56. McClain, "Black People," 81–92.

57. McClain, "Black People," 85–90.

58. Straker, "Black and White and Gray," 27.

delegates? What if the great majority of white Methodists didn't sit on the sidelines during the struggle for black rights and equality? The questions could go on and on.

In reply to these questions and hundreds like them it is difficult to avoid using words like "racist and xenophobic" as Jane Ellen Nickell reminds us.[59] Perhaps it is more appropriate to say, with William McClain, that too readily the Methodists "capitulated to the counter currents of American racist proclivities and yielded to the prevailing morality of the society."[60] Judging the past critically is helpful—but *only* if we can find in that exercise the impetus and tools to do better. The chasm between "Black Lives Matter" and the tacit white supremacy that undergirds many of our social institutions is as apparent as the faces we see in our sanctuaries at 11 a.m. on Sunday morning. It indicates there's still much to do.

FOR FURTHER CONSIDERATION:

1. If we can agree that racial prejudice is a bad thing, how shall we go about overcoming it at both a personal and institutional level? Do you see evidence of white supremacy at work?

2. Our history has seen the deterioration of racial harmony through segregation and the gradual restoration of some harmony through inclusion. What is the lesson to be learned in this?

3. Harry Hosier and Richard Allen represent two rather different alternatives toward a solution to Methodism's dilemma about race. Does either approach seem more tenable today? Why or why not?

4. What alternatives have black Methodists faced historically? Are there parallels and life lessons here for looking at our current situation?

5. Dr. King's statement about his church being "segregated *but not* segregating" is a helpful way of describing the current situation in the church. What steps can you see that would move us toward a more inclusive and less segregated church experience?

59. Nickell, *We Shall Not Be Moved*, 45.
60. McClain, *Black People*, 85.

Chapter 17

"Mutual Rights of Ministers and Members"

Controversy over Shared Governance

THE HISTORY OF METHODISM has been complicated by the fact that it was a movement that accidently became a denomination. Hence, at the very heart of the enterprise there is a tension between its *ad hoc* beginnings and spontaneous spiritual impulses on the one hand, and the Wesleys' love for Anglicanism—with its hierarchy—and their penchant (especially John Wesley's) for order on the other. A push and pull between mutuality and hierarchy, between cooperation and authoritarianism, runs throughout Methodist history.

Methodist authoritarianism was, as Henry Rack pointed out, resident in John Wesley himself. John's "natural authoritarianism and his dominant position in practice are obvious, based on his social status as clergy and his position as long-lived founder of the connexion."[1] The Wesleys' passion for equality and inclusion likely stemmed from their idealistic identification of the Methodist movement as an incarnation of "primitive church." Policies and practices, like classes and annual conferences, were intended as a practical expression of the *koionia* fellowship where "all that believed were together, and had all things in common" (Acts 2:44). But, as Henry Rack noted, "the original implications of free debate and the rights of conscience might seem hard to reconcile with the rigid rules that emerged, largely emanating from Wesley."[2] Miss Marsh, a guest observer at the 1774 Annual

1. Rack, *Works*, X:64.
2. Rack, *Works*, X:64.

Conference, noticed, "Mr. Wesley seemed to do *all* the business himself."[3] John Wesley's critics, both within and beyond the movement, charged him with wielding dictatorial power, and when infrequent clashes over John's decisions occurred there was no court of appeal or redress. His brother Charles reported that he had heard people complaining all over England, that John "ruled with a rod of iron."[4] And on at least one occasion John defended himself to his brother by writing, "I am far from pronouncing my remarks *ex cathedra*."[5] It was a charge that fit well with the often-whispered jibe about "Pope John's" arbitrary power.

When the Conference of 1766 questioned him about his authority, John Wesley replied by reminding them of their beginnings: "In 1744, I wrote to several clergymen, and to all who then served me as sons in the gospel, desiring them to meet me in London, to give me their advice concerning the best method of carrying on the work of God. They did not desire this meeting, but I did, knowing 'in a multitude of counselors there is safety' [Prov 11:14]."[6] John's initial invitation was extended to all the lay preachers associated with the movement, but as the group grew larger, he invited only those preachers with whom he preferred to confer. When the Conference pressed him to explain the basis of his "power," or authority, John took them back to that first meeting he called in November 1738: "Here commenced my power," he explained, "namely a power to appoint when, and where, and how they should meet; and to remove those whose life showed that they had no desire to flee from the wrath to come. And this power remained the same whether the people meeting together were twelve, twelve hundred, or twelve thousand."[7] Wesley thereby argued that by accepting his invitation the attendees placed themselves under his authority for their spiritual improvement and mutual benefit. By issuing the invitation, John placed himself at the head of the movement, as the father "to many sons in the gospel." If his phrasing suggests that John Wesley was sometimes paternalistic—indeed he was.

While John Wesley viewed leadership as a "burden," the preachers often saw it with different eyes than he did. "This is shackling freeborn Englishmen" they said, and demanded "a free Conference, that is, 'a meeting of all the preachers wherein all things shall be determined by most votes.'"[8]

3. J. Wesley, *Journal and Diaries*, V:424n68. Emphasis added.

4. Baker, *Works*, 20:475–76.

5. Campbell, *Works*, 27:315.

6. Rack, *Works*, X:328.

7. Rack, *Works*, X:328.

8. Rack, *Works*, X:328.

John's reply revealed his familiar authoritarian bent when he reminded the preachers they were invited by him, "to *advise*, not *govern* me."[9] Wesley was not prepared to submit his decisions to a vote. He told those preachers who harbored democratic inclinations, "it is possible after my death something of this kind may take place, But not while I live. To *me* the preachers have engaged themselves to submit, to 'serve me as sons in the gospel.' . . . To *me* the people of England in general will submit. But they will not yet submit to any other."[10]

After outliving several designated successors for leadership of the Methodists, John Wesley made an alternate plan to provide stable leadership for the group following the Wesley brothers' demise. The *Deed of Declaration* was drawn up in February 1784, with the help of several solicitors, to satisfy that need.[11] Richard Heitzenrater rightly described it as an "eight-page document, in typical legalese."[12] It was also the "*Magna Carta* of British Methodism" as John Fletcher Hurst described it,[13] because the *Deed of Declaration* invested Wesley's authority in the "Legal One Hundred" hand-picked Methodist preachers he named in the document. "The Legal One Hundred" constituted the Methodist Conference who would, in turn, *elect* their own president and secretary, both of whom were to serve three-year terms. The deed offered fifteen regulations delineating the duties and operations of the Conference, and concluded with stipulations that guaranteed that none of the plan would take effect while either Wesley brother lived.[14]

Rev. Thomas Coke recognized that John Wesley's arbitrary selection of the "Legal One Hundred" would draw further criticism from those preachers who already chafed under his unbridled authority. Nor was it a surprise that the "more cantankerous of the disgruntled preachers" were excluded from Wesley's list. One of them, John Hampson, published a public *Appeal* on behalf of "the excluded ninety-one."[15] John Wesley's response only made the selection seem all the more arbitrary: "In the naming these Preachers, as I had no adviser, so I had no respect of persons; but I simply set down those that, according to the best of my judgment, were most proper."[16] And to those who argued that John Wesley "might have named other Preachers

---

9. Rack, *Works*, X:329. Emphasis original.

10. Rack, *Works*, X:330. Emphasis original.

11. Heitzenrater, *Wesley*, 315–19.

12. Heitzenrater, *Wesley*, 315. Cf. Rack, *Works*, X:949–56.

13. Hurst, *History of British Methodism*, II:971.

14. Rack, *Works*, X:956.

15. Heitzenrater, *Wesley*, 316–17.

16. J. Wesley, *Works of John Wesley* (1872), XIII:249.

instead of these," John quipped, "True, if *I* had thought as well of them as *they* did of themselves."[17] When Hampson's attempt to block adoption of the *Deed of Declaration* at the 1784 Annual Conference failed, he and several others resigned from the movement in protest.[18] The *Deed of Declaration* "did not," as Heitzenrater pointed out, "resolve all the operational issues that were causing tensions from year to year."[19] Later in that same year, in an act that demonstrated his episcopal-like authority over the Methodist movement, John Wesley ordained two of his lay preachers as elders, and elevated Thomas Coke to the office of "superintendent" (or bishop) just before they sailed off to America to give birth to the Methodist Episcopal Church.

Following John Wesley's death in 1791 the Methodist Annual Conference faced three main issues that "had long been shelved under Wesley's benevolent autocracy . . . Methodist leadership; the relations of the preachers and people; and the relation of Methodism with the Church of England. These were not new questions; they had long smoldered, but had been kept beneath the surface of open debate by John Wesley."[20] Over the next three years the leadership question was addressed by a series of untidy proposals, all of which failed, because the Conference was reluctant to place the authority that John Wesley held so long into the hands of any one man, or even a small group of men; and since no women were involved in those conversations their future exclusion from leadership seemed inevitable.

Author unknown. Alexander Kilham (1762–96), an engraving published in *The Primitive Methodist Magazine* (1926/27) with the caption: "The Rev. Alexander Kilham, First Methodist Reformer and A Pioneer of Representative Government." https://www.myunitedmethodists.org.uk/content/people/ministers/alexander-kilham-his-influence-on-christian-democracy.

The *Plan of Pacification* was formulated in 1795 as an attempt to strike a truce between "the Church Methodists" who wanted to maintain the movement's traditional connection to the COE and the "radicals" who wanted the independence of a new denomination and sacramental authority for the preachers. This plan decentralized the leadership by allowing the trustees and stewards of the various Methodist chapels to decide whether or not lay preachers would be permitted to administer the sacraments in their sanctuaries. In truth, however,

17. J. Wesley, *Works of John Wesley* (1872), XIII:249–50. Emphasis added.
18. Heitzenrater, *Wesley*, 316–17.
19. Heitzenrater, *Wesley*, 317.
20. Walsh, "Methodism at the End," I:278.

the *Plan of Pacification* pacified almost no one. It caused the Church Methodists to be branded as schismatics by their fellow Anglicans, and to the "radicals," like lay preacher Alexander Kilham (1762–98), it seemed like still another act of "tyranny." He promptly published a barrage of protests. Kilham explained, "In all the pamphlets I have published this year, I have one object in view. That is, to show that our people labor under an oppressive system of rules of discipline, which does not admit their having any share in the government of the Connexion, but by the good will of an affiliant [of "the Legal One Hundred"]; and this is not of necessity in him, but of choice."[21] The controversy that ensued was so intense that the Connection moderated the *Plan of Pacification* the following year. It also brought charges against Alexander Kilham and expelled him.

The *Plan of Pacification* completed the British Methodists' gradual separation from the COE. As Robert Tucker observed, "After the terms of the *Plan of Pacification* and *The Regulations of Leeds* went into effect, one is not correct in thinking that either temperamentally or sociologically the Methodists were part of the Established Church. There was, to be sure, no formal declaration of the severance of relationships with the Established Church; but the separation was an accomplished fact."[22] Another result was that Kilham and other like-minded Methodists founded the Methodist New Connection in 1797. The New Connection differed from the parent body in their inclusion of laity representatives in the deliberations of both their annual and general conferences. When the Kilhamites took the name "Connection," the Wesleyan Methodists embraced their new identity as the Wesleyan Methodist Church and signaled that the Methodist movement in England was well on its way to becoming an institutional church.

Following John Wesley's death, the Wesleyan Methodist Conference was led by "six sagacious pilot presidents,"[23] but it was Jabez Bunting (1779–1858) who gave formal shape and identity to the Wesleyan Methodist Church as it distanced itself from the COE on the one hand, and distinguished itself from revivalistic enthusiasm on the

Photo by David Octavius Hill, *Rev. Jabez Bunting,* **circa 1843–47, public domain.**

21. Kilham, *Account of the Trial*, iv.

22. Tucker, *Separation of the Methodists*, 172–73.

23. Hurst, *History of British Methodism*, III:111–12.

other hand. Under Bunting's leadership the movement became a church with proper order and discipline. When the great Mow Cop revivals of 1807 sent droves of enthusiastic converts streaming into the Wesleyan Methodist Church tensions emerged between the new variety of "church Methodists" and those who longed for the movement's revivalist beginnings. In 1810, the Primitive Methodist Society was established as a home for the revivalists and it was soon followed by the Bible Christians, who emerged in Cornwall under the leadership of Methodist preacher Willian O'Bryan in 1815. All three of the early secessionist groups retained Wesleyan theology and ethos, but the Primitive Methodists and the Bible Christians developed church polities that stressed shared governance among clergy and laity, which reflected the earlier days when Methodism was a movement, and not a church.

American Methodism struggled with issues of identity and leadership style almost from the outset. The MEC was born at the Christmas Conference of 1784, when Thomas Coke, an Anglican priest who had recently and illegally been ordained as a Methodist "Superintendent" by John Wesley, arrived at Lovely Lane Chapel, near Baltimore, to ordain Francis Asbury (1745–1816) as a Methodist deacon, priest, and superintendent on successive days. Wesley avoided using the word "ordain" to describe his actions, he preferred to say "commissioned." He intended Coke and Asbury to use the term "superintendent," but upon arriving in America they preferred the title "bishop" instead.[24]

Artist unknown, image made by GS 1832, *Rev. William O' Bryan*, public domain.

British-born Francis Asbury took the pulse of the American preachers among whom he had served so long and insisted he be elected by a vote prior to his ordination as bishop. It was a rare concession to the republican "consent of the governed" spirit that so much shaped the tenor of the times.[25] But some preachers, like James O'Kelly (1736?–1826), questioned whether that election took place: "We had episcopacy, but not bishop," he wrote. "Thomas and Francis were our superintendents, as president elders; according to John's appointment. But they were not elected by the suffrage of the conference, although it is so

24. Lee, *Short History of the Methodists*, 87–88, preserves John Wesley's programmatic letter.

25. Lee, *Short History of the Methodists*, 89.

written in the book of discipline."[26] Observers reported that Asbury had been ordained as a "superintendent" and only insisted upon being called "bishop" after that fact, and O'Kelly point-

ed to a communication from Asbury in 1787 as evidence for his assertion.[27] Jesse Lee, in his *Short History of the Methodists*, asserted that Bishop Asbury also altered the published minutes of the 1784 Confer-ence to reflect the more authoritarian no-menclature throughout.[28]

Early American Methodism was riven by several conflicting issues that would not be resolved easily: Loyalist or Patriot? Slavery or Abolition? Hierarchical or Equalitarian? Was the organization and style of leadership of the new church going to be Federalist—stressing strong central authority—or Republican—embracing the rhetoric of personal liberty and equal-ity that had given birth to the new na-tion? Elizabeth Georgian captured these tensions when she described "A Church in Crisis? [due to the] Paradoxes in the Rise of American Methodism."[29] By the time American Methodism transitioned

Benjamin Tanner, *The Rev'd Francis Asbury, Bishop of the Methodist Episcopal Church in the United States*, Philadelphia, 1814. An engraving made from the portrait by John Paradise, in the Library of Congress Prints and Photographs Division Washington, DC, 20540, item no. 1.237.077.

from being a movement among immigrant people to the formal establish-ment of the MEC in 1784, Francis Asbury had emerged as "the father of American Methodism." While Asbury was aided by many American "sons in the gospel," he was the driving hand and galvanizing influence behind the Methodist movement becoming a church. His herculean efforts and frenetic ministry mirrored that of his mentor and hero, John Wesley, and in his passive-aggressive autocratic style Asbury may have even eclipsed the movement's founder.

Even among pious people committed to a common cause the task of forming a spontaneous movement into an institutional church brought controversy and contention. Much of the early contention revolved around

26. O'Kelly, *Author's Apology*, 11.

27. O'Kelly, *Author's Apology*, 13.

28. Lee, *Short History of the Methodists*, 125.

29. Georgian, "Church in Crisis?"

the question of the lay preachers' administration of the sacraments in the physical absence of ordained clergy. James O'Kelly's sympathetic biographer reported: "At the conference of 1773, in which Mr. Asbury's spirit ruled, some rules were passed to avoid administering the ordinances, and also regarding attendance upon the Episcopal Church. The conference was held with closed doors, a thing not relished by the liberty loving Americans."[30] Nor did O'Kelly think "Mr. Asbury's rule for a layman to 'pay, pray, and obey,' never yet appealed to free citizens in a free country," as he said.[31]

When debate over the question of the lay preachers administering the sacraments was postponed again at the 1778 Methodist Annual Conference the Virginia preachers met separately at Fluvanna Country on May 18, 1779, to resolve the matter.[32] After they created a "presbytery" among themselves, and authorized their own sacramental ministry (not unlike John Wesley's solution devised in ordinations for Americans in 1784), the Annual Conference of 1780 passed a disciplinary resolution against the Fluvanna brethren, and the wayward Methodist preachers were cajoled and bullied back in line by the northern preachers, led by Asbury.[33] But, as Dee Andrews pointed out, "the sacramental controversy—ostensibly a struggle over the powers of Methodist ministry but [was also] a cultural contest between Strawbridge's democratic Irish Methodism and Asbury's loyalty to Wesley's authoritarian 'old plan'—[the struggle] continued unsatisfactorily resolved for four years."[34] Although there were many voices raised in the contention between those who held federalist and republican governmental sentiments in early American Methodism, the strife that emerged between the Methodist preacher James O'Kelly and Bishop Francis Asbury epitomized the controversy.

James O'Kelly had been born in Ireland and emigrated to Virginia at an early age. There he experienced religious awakening in 1774, perhaps through the efforts of Robert Strawbridge, and a call to ministry; he received a license to preach the next year. After preaching as an itinerant for

Artist unknown, *James O'Kelly (1735–1826),* **in** *North Carolina History Encyclopedia,* **public domain.**

30. MacClenny, *Life of O'Kelly,* 32.

31. MacClenny, *Life of O'Kelly,* 32–33.

32. MacClenny, *Life of O'Kelly,* 33.

33. Norwood, *Story of American Methodism,* 91–92.

34. Andrews, *Methodists in Revolutionary America,* 64.

nearly a decade, James O'Kelly was ordained as a deacon by Dr. Coke at the Christmas Conference in 1784. O'Kelly opposed a series of measures Bishop Asbury proposed, which, in O'Kelly's mind, reeked of authoritarian control. His disenchantment with Asbury's leadership began in 1787 with his push to have Richard Whatcoat ordained as a third "Superintendent," as well as Asbury's insistence that all the preachers should address him as "Bishop."[35] After a series of letters and at least one heated conversation over the plan of governance, James concluded: "I now began to discover the rapid five years of growth of 'a moderate Episcopacy.' Whereunto shall I liken it; it is like unto a dwarf whose head grows too fast for his body."[36]

At the 1792 General Council the revisions to the MEC *Discipline* were introduced and debated for nearly three days. Although the real debate was still about federalism verses republicanism, the conversation reached the breaking point over the question of whether any preacher had the right to appeal his appointment or "stationing," as it was called then. The republicans wanted the right of approval, and the federalists—those who wanted a stronger episcopacy—did not. The protests were often registered in the political vernacular of the new republic, but when the vote was taken the republicans had lost their cause. Timothy Allen's succinct summary is apt: "1792, O'Kelly and Asbury quarreled over itinerants assignments. After Francis Asbury and Dr. Thomas Coke publically humiliated and betrayed him in the battle, James O'Kelly left the Methodists in 1793 and formed the Republican Methodists in August 1794."[37]

The issues that caused contention between Asbury and O'Kelly were many. It is clear, for example, that O'Kelly arrived in America with a political republicanism hard learned in the context of British colonial occupation of Ireland. He quickly associated Asbury's imperious ecclesiastical attitude with his Britishness: "Francis was born and nurtured in the land of kings," James wrote, "that which is bred in the bone, is hard to be got of the flesh."[38] Asbury also sat out the American War for Independence, while O'Kelly served in the Virginia militia.[39] And just as the MEC began backing away from its abolitionist roots, James O'Kelly, who had manumitted at least one slave upon receiving Christ into his life, published the abolitionist *Essay on Negro Slavery* (1789).[40]

35. O'Kelly, *Author's Apology*, 11.

36. O'Kelly, *Author's Apology*, 19.

37. Allen, "'Some Expectation of Being Promoted,'" 63.

38. O'Kelly, Author's *Apology*, 21.

39. Andrews, *Methodists in Revolutionary America*, 202.

40. Georgian, "That Unhappy Division," 220–21.

Commentators also rightly detect that O'Kelly's challenges to Asbury's episcopal authority quickly became more of a clash of personalities and point of view between Asbury and O'Kelly than about what was best for Methodism's mission. Jessie Lee reported that O'Kelly's opposition to the council plan was due to personal ambition.[41] John Wigger suspected "for all his populism, O'Kelly craved personal recognition."[42] The strife over Francis Asbury's "unbridled authority" deeply impacted Asbury as well. The bishop seemed to be defending his leadership style in a letter Asbury wrote just a few weeks before his death: "the commonality of the people really do suppose that a bishop is a tyrant, the same as a pope, dreadful, dangerous creatures," he wrote. "With us a bishop is a plain man, altogether like his brethren, wearing no marks of distinction . . . raised to a small degree of constituted and elective authority above all his brethren; and in the executive department, power to say, 'Brother, that must not be, that cannot be,' having full power to put a negative or a positive in his high charge of administration."[43] Asbury saw himself in a much different light than others, like James O'Kelly saw him.

Francis Asbury also seemed unable to disassociate leadership of the MEC from his person as bishop and he believed that submission to the authority of the bishop was to be a spiritual virtue among the Methodists. His spiritualized interpretation of the MEC crisis in governance emerged in Asbury's *Causes, Evils, and Cures of Heart and Church Divisions—Extracted from the Works of Burroughs and Baxter* (1792). He was willing to attribute the conflicts with Strawbridge and O'Kelly to each man's inordinate pride, since "Pride is the greatest master of misrule in the world. It is the greatest incendiary in the soul of man, in families, in towns, in cities, in all societies, in church and state. . . . Pride is the ringleader to all riots, divisions, disturbances among us."[44] He framed the controversy in terms of personal relationship, not institutional governance or organizational structure.

Deliberations about governance continued in earnest as the MEC began to take an institutional character that its growing role as a national church seemed to require. The career and efforts of Rev. Nathan Bangs (1778–1862) epitomized the MEC's march toward respectability and "officialdom."[45] His reflections on the debate about governance at the 1812 General Council summarized well the tension between "two opposite views

---

41. Lee, *Short History of the Methodists*, 157.

42. Wigger, *American Saint*, 215.

43. Asbury, *Journal and Letters*, III:544–45.

44. Asbury, *Causes, Evils, and Cures*, 7.

45. Hatch, *Democratization of American Christianity*, 201–6.

of the doctrine of responsibility" that had been with the movement from its very beginnings: "The former traced responsibility from the General Conference, who made the regulations and judged of episcopal acts, to the episcopacy; and thence down through the several grades of church officers; the latter traced it up through the societies, to quarterly and annual conferences, to the General Conference."[46]

It is at least a little ironic that Nicholas Snethen (1769–1845), the young preacher whom Bishop Asbury enlisted to write against James

O'Kelly in 1800,[47] emerged as the MEC's chief clergy advocate for "mutual rights" and lay inclusion in the governance of MEC in the 1820s. Equally ironic was the way in which a church which was so completely connected to episcopal authority and hierarchy could successfully market itself as a populist movement and ride the crest of the wave of "Jacksonian populism" that swept across the land.[48] As Elizabeth Georgian noted, "The men who led the church so skillfully blurred the line between a church for the people and an American church, that their contemporaries and historians alike saw the Methodist Episcopal Church as democratic despite the underlying reality."[49] These internal disputes about shared leadership occurred at the very same time that Methodists of African descent were being segregated away from the Methodist mainstream, and women were being systematically excluded from leadership roles; shared governance, or, more correctly, the lack

Artist unknown, *Nicholas Snethen, 1769–1845*, in T. H. Colhouer, Sketches of the Founders of the Methodist Protestant Church (Pittsburgh: MPC Publishing Concern, 1880), from The Internet Archive, public domain.

thereof, impacted the MEC at many levels.

William Stockton was a printer and MEC layman who gave both voice and name to the cause of shared governance when he established the newspaper *The Mutual Rights of Ministers and Members of the Methodist Episcopal Church* (1824). Employing white-hot rhetoric, Stockton argued that the MEC's hierarchal approach was both unchristian and un-American: "no form of church government is adapted to our state of society, but such as one

46. Bangs, *History of the Methodist Episcopal Church,* II:195.

47. Snethen, *Reply to an Apology.*

48. Hatch, *Democratization of American Christianity,* 17–49.

49. Georgian, "Church in Crisis?," 10.

as will promote the general prosperity, by securing the rights and promoting the prosperity of each individual," he urged.[50] Rev. Nicholas Snethen was one of the few ordained MEC ministers to actively take up the cause of *Mutual Rights* for the laity and for the lay "local preachers" who out-numbered the ordained clergy three to one. A traveling associate of Bishop Asbury who had nicknamed him "the silver trumpet" due to his preaching ability, Snethen wrote against the renegade James O'Kelly in 1800. But by 1814, Nicholas had become a vocal advocate for more inclusive governance in the MEC.[51] He recognized that the local preachers and lay class leaders, who were not permitted to participate in governance, were actually the backbone of the MEC and therefore deserved a place at the "table" of decision making. "Such advocacy," Richey et al. pointed out, "involved risk, particularly for preachers under appointment."[52]

The MEC General Conferences of 1820 and 1824 ignored and then stonewalled the campaign and many petitions for "mutual rights." Eventually the threat of expulsion was added to the Conference's replies in an attempt to curtail controversy by silencing the reformers. Knee-deep in the struggle for mutual rights, Rev. Snethen pointed out that the very manner in which the pleas for mutual rights had been treated demonstrated exactly *why* reform was so sorely needed. He wrote, "From the day they expel the friends of lay representation they shall give a direction and impulse to all their movements . . . to prevent an internal revolution; but great and important changes in the practical operations of their discipline must be inevitable."[53] In 1827, the Baltimore Annual Conference expelled several of its clergy members for their harsh rhetoric and divisive actions on behalf of "mutual rights." These actions, as well as a large number of petitions and resolutions, made shared governance one of the main topics at the MEC General Conference of 1828.[54] When the "mutual rights" petitions and resolutions were read out, they met roughly the same cold indifference that met Orange Scott and the abolitionist reformers a decade later.

The only appropriate resolution to "the unhappy excitement that has existed in some parts of our work"[55] foreseen by the 1828 MEC General Conference was for their membership to either disavow the sentiments expressed in *Mutual Rights* or leave the MEC. The reformers refused to accept

50. Richey et al., *Methodist Experience,* II:203.

51. Simpson, *Cyclopedia of Methodism,* 812–13.

52. Richey et al., *Methodist Experience,* I:167.

53. Snethen, *Lay Representation,* ix.

54. Simpson, *Cyclopedia of Methodism,* 602–3.

55. Richey et al., *Methodist Experience,* II:214.

the resolution, withdrew from the Conference, and called a meeting of their own in Baltimore for November 12, 1828. They drafted a new constitution, discipline, and hymnbook, and gave birth to the Methodist Protestant Church (MPC). The MPC was a Methodist church whose governance was based on congregational polity and shared governance among clergy and laity; it was no accident that the word "Episcopal" disappeared from its name. When the new MPC was inaugurated on November 2, 1830, it was comprised of eighty former MEC ministers and more than 5, 000 congregants.[56] The path to full inclusion of both laymen and laywomen was a long and difficult one for the MEC. In 1872, lay*men* were first elected and admitted to the deliberations of the Methodist General Conference.[57] But in 1888, five notable Methodist women were elected as delegates and sent to the General Conference; however, as was reported in chapter 15, they were refused participation as voting delegates. As Frederick Norwood reported, "The Northern church was not yet ready for equal representation (only two from each annual conference [at General Conference]), nor was it ready to open the annual conference to laypersons. Only with the turn of the century did equal representation arrive, and participation in the annual conference not until 1932."[58]

The journey toward inclusion is not over yet, as lay pastors and bivocational ministers, who are doing most of the church's parish work in many regions, feel they have earned a greater voice in governance. And as the UMC and other Wesleyan churches live into the twenty-first century, increasingly larger numbers of people, the so-called "nones," question the validity of the institutional church, while many others have become nonparticipants, describing themselves as "spiritual but not religious" (SBNR), due to ecclesial exclusion and *rigor mortis*. SBNR people have not given up on spirituality, but they are giving upon churches they do not find to be inclusive and welcoming.[59] Leadership style and shared governance play a large role in validating their experience.

FOR FURTHER CONSIDERATION:

1. Has our approach to governance helped or hindered the cause of the gospel in the UMC? How? Why?

---

56. Richey et al., *Methodist Experience*, II:214.

57. Richey et al., *Methodist Experience*, II:214; see II:31 for photos of them.

58. Norwood, *Story of American Methodism*, 258.

59. See, for example, Duekson and Richardson, "Learning."

2. Is there a workable way to achieve a balance point between a stable organizational structure and spontaneity when it comes to institutional leadership and function?

3. Is it more difficult for individuals or for institutions to be morally courageous? Why?

4. Someone, perhaps Winston Churchill, quipped that generals always prepare "to fight the last war" (implying it would be far wiser to prepare for the next one). Is this true of the church? If so, how can that dilemma be resolved?

5. Are there resources in our past and our heritage that can help us prepare for a better future? What shape or function will the church of the future need to take in order to be relevant, inclusive, and meet the needs of God's people?

CHAPTER 18

"Persons of Sacred Worth"

Controversy over Full Inclusion of LGBTQ People

THE HISTORY OF CHRISTIANS and their churches' interaction with gay and lesbian people has been another one of those sagas that has been written by "the victors." Too often the story has been often told in tones of prejudice, exclusion, and hatred; sometimes it has been written in blood. This inconvenient truth is reflected in the sad fact that "faggot," a derogatory euphemism for queer people, stems directly from an archaic name for the bundle of twigs that kindled bonfires to extinguish their lives along with those of other social "undesirables" like religious heretics, "wise women" (witches), and Jews.[1]

It is easy enough to trace some of this abominable treatment of gay people to interpretations of the Scriptures, which carry harsh denunciations of them. Leviticus 20:13, for example, voices a murderous antipathy: "if a man lies with a male as with a woman, both of them have committed *an abomination*, they shall be put to death; their blood is upon them" (NRSV). Same-sex relationships were described as "an abomination" in the Levitical holiness code. But dozens of other practices—like eating with foreigners, failing to keep the kosher dietary laws (no rare meat, bacon, shrimp, or lobster, etc.), going near "unclean" things like a pregnant or menstruating woman, a dead body, or failing to wash one's hands before eating—were all considered "abominations." In turn, unspeakable abominations were committed against LBGTQ people for two millennia based on a prejudicial

---

1. *Oxford English Dictionary*, s.v. "faggot (n. and adj.)," https://www.oed.com/viewdictionaryentry/Entry/67623.

reading of this one segment of the Levitical "holiness code" and treating it as normative practice for all times and places.

Cultural conditioning (both ancient and modern) also played a significant role in the interpretation of the narrative in Genesis 19, which has often been read as a saga of God's judgment and destruction of Sodom because of its residents' practice of same-sex unions and their evil intent to gang-rape angelic visitors lodged in the house of Lot. Hence, "Sodomite" became a common euphemism for "homosexual" (as in 1 Tim 1:10, KJV).[2] Modern research, however, pioneered by D. S. Bailey (1955), recognized that the OT text's censure of the men of Sodom had more to do with their flagrant violation of the hospitality code that undergirded Middle Eastern culture than it had to do with sexuality *per se*.[3] As UMC biblical scholar Richard Hays said succinctly, "The notorious story of Sodom and Gomorrah—often cited in connection with homosexuality—is actually irrelevant to the topic."[4]

Of the three New Testament passages that are traditionally understood to censure gay and lesbian relationships, two (1 Cor 6:9 and 1 Tim 1:10) employ terms in the *koine* Greek that are rare enough to make their exact meaning the focus of considerable scholarly debate. Since the terms could be translated as "effeminate" (as in the KJV), some modern commentators, like Walter Wink, suggest the translation of the passage as explicitly referring to "homosexuals" is an overreach since the meaning of the terms is simply "ambiguous,"[5] while others like Robert Gagnon strongly disagree.[6] The third New Testament passage, Romans 1:26–27, includes same-sex relationships on a long list of "improper conduct" epitomizing human waywardness.[7] The exegesis that defines gay and lesbian relationships as "against nature," based on Romans 1:26–27 was popularized by Augustine (354–430) though others interpreted the "improper conduct" mentioned in the text as referring to heterosexual people acting like gay people.[8] Thomas Aquinas (1225–75)

2. *Oxford English Dictionary,* s.v. "Sodomite," https://www.oed.com.ezp.lib.rochester.edu/ view/Entry/183881?redirectedFrom=Sodomite#eid. The term was rarely used before the seventeenth century.

3. Bailey, *Homosexuality*, 50ff.

4. Hays, "Biblical Witness," 65.

5. Wink, *Homosexuality and the Bible*, 1. See also Scroggs, *New Testament*, 29–65.

6. Gagnon, *Bible and Homosexual Practice*, 303–40.

7. See Romans 1:28–31: "And since they did not see fit to acknowledge God, God gave them up to a base mind and to improper conduct. They were filled with all manner of wickedness, evil, covetousness, malice. Full of envy, murder, strife, deceit, malignity, they are gossips, slanderers, haters of God, insolent, haughty, boastful, inventors of evil, disobedient to parents, foolish, faithless, heartless, ruthless."

8. Boswell, *Christianity, Social Tolerance, and Homosexuality*, 147–49, on Augustine's exegesis; and Townsly, "Queer Sects," 56–79.

solidified the connection between the exclusion of gay people and the "against nature" exegesis of Romans 1:26–27, but Aquinas also noted that there was moral ambiguity attached to the notion of assigning blame to "an unnatural act," which seemed to be completely "natural" for some people.[9] Setting the Romans 1:26–27 passage in the larger context of the Scripture's teachings about gendered relationships, marriage, and procreation, a "canonical context," UMC New Testament scholar Richard Hays concluded, "[indicates] the biblical witness against homosexual practices is univocal."[10] Other scholars, like Walter Wink, disagree and urge an interpretive process "provided by a critique of domination [with which] we are able to filter out the sexism, partriarchalism, violence, and homophobia that are very much a part of the Bible, thus liberating it to reveal to us in fresh ways the inbreaking, in our time, of God's domination-free order."[11]

Of the five Bible passages that have traditionally been interpreted as condemning same-sex relationships, the modern application of four of them seems to be indeterminate. This seems like a rather slim witness upon which to hang the long history of exclusion and persecution of queer people. In this regard, it seems necessary to consider why Western culture, and Christians in particular, have used the Bible as either a reason or an excuse to exclude, hate, and harm gay people, since weaponizing the Bible against them runs counter to the prevailing tone of both Testaments. The Scriptures persistently urge the faithful to care for "the other," whether they are the widow, orphans, or the stranger (Deut 10:17–19; Jas 1:27). Moses (Lev 19:18) and Jesus Christ (Matt 19:19; 22:39) spoke with one voice as they urged "Love your neighbor as yourself." But as we have seen (in previous chapters), the Bible's words have been used in prejudicial ways to silence women and exclude them from religious leadership, and to enslave people of African descent. These historical examples may cause us to reasonably conclude that prejudice (conscious or otherwise) has been at work in the way the Bible has been used against LGBTQ people.

Looking back over a long history of intolerance, John Boswell noted, "Beginning about 1150, for reasons I cannot adequately explain, there was a great upsurge in popular intolerance of gay people. There was also at this time violent outbursts against Jews, Muslims, and witches. Women were suddenly excluded from power structures to which they had previously had access."[12] What persecuted groups had in common was the fact that they did

---

9. Boswell, *Christianity, Social Tolerance, and Homosexuality,* 303–32.

10. Hays, "Biblical Witness," 73.

11. Wink, *Homosexuality and the Bible,* 48.

12. Boswell, "Church and the Homosexual," 6–7.

not fit well in the medieval mainstream, and for that they were "othered" by a fearful society.[13] Lumping LGBTQ people together with heretics, Jews, witches, gypsies, and the Knights Templar as objects of derision and persecution evidences that "a considerable transformation of public attitudes toward homosexual behavior [also] took place during the later twelfth and thirteenth centuries."[14] Other historians, however, like R. W. Southern, posit a more persistent pattern of gay exclusion and persecution throughout the entire medieval period.[15]

The sixteenth-century Protestant reformers continued what was, by then, the traditional interpretation that linked sodomy and Romans 1:26–27. Martin Luther, for example, wrote: "the heinous conduct of the people of Sodom is . . . altogether contrary to nature. Whence comes this perversity? Undoubtedly from Satan."[16] There was a slight decline in public hostility toward queer people during the Georgian "century of sex" (see chapter 10), but there was no evidence that the Methodists contributed to that development. "Buggery," as a male same-sex act was called in popular parlance, was still punishable by death in Georgian England. Although the London newspapers report twenty-eight arrests for "buggery" between 1721–23, the accused person was generally fined, consigned to the pillory, and imprisoned (up to six months).[17] Molly Houses, like "Mother Clap's" in Field Land, Holborn, London, were broadly known and well frequented by gay men. In February of 1726, "Mother Clap's" was raided by "a squadron of police constables" and forty men were "rounded up and hauled off to Newgate prison to await trial." Of the accused, "most of them were set free due to lack of evidence. A number of them, however, were fined, imprisoned, and exhibited in the pillory, and three men were subsequently hanged at Tyburn."[18] Notable gay men, like Horatio Walploe, Fourth Earl of Oxford and son of the Prime Minister, lived a productive, quasi-closeted life,[19] while others like "the Arse Bishop Joelin" (Bishop of Clougher, Percy Joyceln) were exposed,

13. "'Othering' is described as a social process whereby a dominant group or person uses negative attributes to define and subordinate others. Literature suggests othering creates exclusive relationships and puts patients at risk for suboptimal care" (Roberts and Schiavenato, "Othering in the Nursing Context," 174–81).

14. Boswell, *Christianity, Social Tolerance and Homosexuality*, 301.

15. Southern, *St. Anselm*, 148–50, disagreed, arguing: "The author has collected a mass of material with some important discussions, and . . . with misconceptions which vitiate many of his conclusions" (148).

16. Pelikan, *Luther's Works*, 3:255.

17. Norton, "Newspaper Reports."

18. Norton, *Mother Clap's Molly House*.

19. Artlark, "Gay Georgian London."

critiqued, and lampooned by the popular press as is evidenced by Robert Cruikshank's cartoon: "Do as I say, Not as I do."[20]

Robert Cruikshank, *Arse Bishop Jocelyn and a Soldier* (1822), **public domain.**

If the Wesley brothers were aware of the gay subculture, or the "Molly Houses" of eighteenth-century London, they made no mention of it. "Sodomites" appeared twice in John Wesley's sermons, each time as one item among many in a long list of the failings of "the children of disobedience," but without special comment or condemnation.[21] Wesley's *Notes* on the Genesis 19 Sodom account likened the plight of those ministering angels with crises faced by Methodist itinerant preachers—both of whom were

20. See also, the Robert Pierpont Library, where it is displayed: "Print shows a backroom in the White Lion public house in Westminster where the Bishop of Clogher, Percy Jocelyn, and a private in uniform have been apprehended 'in flagrante delicto' by a constable, who has seized the two men by the neck. Bishop Jocelyn is saying: 'Do let me go I'll give you £500,' while the constable replies: 'Oh no I'll make a full exposure so come to the black hole and you shall cast lots again, Old File.' The soldier, his trouser undone, cries: 'Oh! I am ruin'd and undone.' A group of spectators who have gathered in the doorway of the room at right are shouting: 'Hang the dogs I say let them not disgrace our gallant soldiers shoot the beasts'; 'They must not live to disgrace the Church and the Army'; 'Send them to Hell or Turkey'; 'Send them to China'; 'The Pillory The Pillory'; 'Hang them in Chains.'" http://commons.wikimedia.org/wikiFile:Percy_Jocelyn_Bishop_of_Clogher_by_Cruikshank.jpg.

21. J. Wesley, *Sermons*, II:67–68; J. Wesley, *Works* (1872), X:367–77.

attacked by angry mobs. The lamentable aspect of the event, as Wesley saw it, was twofold: there was no magistrate willing to help them, and in sending out his daughters to be assaulted by the mob Lot felt forced to decide between two evil alternatives. "It is true," Wesley wrote, "of two evils we must choose the less, but of two sins we must choose neither, nor ever do evil that good may come of it." Ironically, Wesley censored Lot's cowardice and not the "sodomites" who occasioned it.[22]

John Wesley's published comment on Romans 1:26–27 followed Augustine and Martin Luther by describing the "unnatural" use of human desires and bodies as "dishonour to the body, as their idolatry was to God."[23] His commentary on 1 Corinthians 6:9 viewed the list of vices, which are said to exclude a person from the kingdom of God, as a clear warning that something relatively minor, like (following the KJV) being "*effeminate*," that is, living "an easy, indolent way, taking up no cross, enduring no hardship," invariably leads to greater sins "since every one is a step toward hell."[24] Following the KJV translation of the controversial term as "effeminate" instead of using "sodomite" or "homosexual," Wesley considered "sodomy" as ranking among the "greatest sins" but once again did not single it out for special critique or condemnation.[25]

Tracing the history of gay people in premodern America is very difficult because aversion, persecution, and the potential of violence against them caused gay people to make themselves as invisible as possible. As Colin Talley noted: "Buggery in the barn was not the sort of thing that would tend to be recorded for posterity and it would not reach the courts if the sexual partners could help it."[26] The American oppression of queer people, like the oppression of people of African descent and indigenous people, can be traced to the unholy alliance between Christianity and British Colonialism. English legislation oppressing gay people reached back to a series of "Buggery Acts" that began in 1533. As Asal and Sommer explained, "when the system of [British] Common Law was transported worldwide with British colonialism, the sodomy provision traveled alongside that corpus. In sum, it was a combination of common law, statutory law, and judicial and legal scholarship that together helped criminalize sodomy throughout the expanding British Empire."[27] British Buggery Acts remained in effect until

22. J. Wesley, *Explanatory Notes,* I:76–77.

23. J. Wesley, *Explanatory Notes,* III:364.

24. J. Wesley, *Explanatory Notes,* III:418–19.

25. J. Wesley, *Explanatory Notes,* III:418–19.

26. Talley, "Gender and Male Same-Sex Erotic Behavior," 385.

27. Asal and Sommer, *Legal Path Dependence,* 41.

1861, when imprisonment replaced the death penalty; the amended law survived until 1967.[28]

The British Buggery Acts were replicated all across colonial America as "Sodomy Laws" that were enforced with greater and lesser degrees of enthusiasm. Puritan New England was a particularly dangerous place to be charged with sodomy since, as Edmund Morgan reported, "Sodomy, to be sure, they usually punished with death; but rape, adultery, and fornication they regarded as pardonable human weakness.[29] With American independence the death penalty gradually disappeared from sodomy laws in all thirteen states, but same-sex relations (along with various other kinds of sex acts) were still deemed criminal offenses and were liable to result in prosecution.[30] In 1778, for example, the fair-minded Thomas Jefferson suggested castration instead of death as a more suitable penalty for "rape, polygamy, or sodomy."[31]

State sodomy statutes multiplied as new states joined the nation. They varied significantly in their severity; while the criminalization of LGBTQ people was uniform, the enforcement of sodomy laws was not. As Margot Canaday reported: "those laws were maintained into the nineteenth century, when they were used in cases in which the sex enacted was either violent or extremely public, police rarely enforced sodomy laws against anyone before 1880, even when such illegal activities were notorious in the community."[32] The looser morals ushered in by the modern era, as in the Roaring Twenties, caused a cultural backlash that included the expansion of sodomy laws as well as their more aggressive enforcement.[33] This development was described by Mark Smith as a transition "from invisibility to pathology" in which "homosexuality" was described as "a sexual perversion" in governmental documents and as a "sociopathic personality disturbance" by the American Psychiatric Association (1952).[34] This was the social climate in which many of mainline Protestantism's official assessments of queer people were formulated.

Attitudes toward LGBTQ people once again began to change during the tumultuous 1960s, as looser social mores made the gay subculture more visible to the general public at the same time that African Americans,

28. "Law In England," 3.

29. Morgan, "Puritans and Sex," 603.

30. Canaday, "We Colonials."

31. "Amendment VIII."

32. Canaday, "We Colonials," 3–4.

33. Canaday, "We Colonials," 4. .

34. Smith, *Secular Faith*, 99.

women, Latinos, and Indigenous people also pressed for civil rights and equal opportunity. But sodomy laws still kept many LGBTQ people "in the closet," because they would be exposed both to social stigma and potential punishment if they lived openly. In this challenging context "the initial stirrings for Gay Rights began."[35] The six days of protest and riots that erupted after a violent police raid on the Stonewall, a gay bar in New York City, on June 28, is viewed as the catalyst for the modern Gay Rights Movement. The obvious parallels between the struggles of black, brown, and red peoples, as well as women, for full equality in America placed the plight of LGBTQ people in a broader social context and greater public awareness about their plight gradually led to greater tolerance. These changing attitudes were reflected in the decriminalization of same-sex expression between consenting adults, on a state-by-state basis, as well as in the US Supreme Court, ruling all laws that discriminate on the basis of "sexual orientation" are unconstitutional (2003). In twelve states, however, sodomy laws remain on the books and are used to harass LGBTQ people.[36]

Sexual tolerance was fueled by new strides in scientific and social science research, beginning with groundbreaking work by leading psychologists like Dr. Evelyn Hooker (1907–96). Hooker's "The Adjustment of the Male Homosexual" (1957) showed that previous studies, which led to the classification of "homosexuality" as a "mental or personality disorder,"[37] were fundamentally flawed. After decades of further research and discussion, the American Psychiatric Association (APA) removed "homosexuality" from its listing of *Diagnostic and Statistical Manual of Mental Disorders* in 1973. The APA's official finding was: "The longstanding consensus of the behavioral and social sciences and the health and mental health professions is that homosexuality *per se* is a normal and positive variation of human sexual orientation." Since 1974, the APA "has opposed stigma, prejudice, discrimination, and violence [against people] based in sexual orientation and has taken a leadership role in supporting the equal rights of lesbian, gay, and bisexual individuals."[38] A seminal study by the prestigious *New England Journal of Medicine* concluded: "The origin of sexual orientation appears to be multifactorial and diverse"; that is to say that gay and lesbian people are formed by the same combination of psychological and biological factors (like genetics, hormones, and brain function, etc.) that straight

35. Smith, *Secular Faith*, 100–104.

36. Villarreal, "Sodomy Laws."

37. Compton et al., "Introduction," 1.

38. "Resolution on Appropriate Affirmative Responses." The original statement is replete with references to published research that supports the resolution. These have been removed for readability.

people are.[39] These assessments caused many contemporary Christians to recognize that LGBTQ life is not a moral failing or mental disorder as had long been assumed and argued.

These developments in modern culture and the social sciences were mirrored in biblical scholarship. Beginning with the work of D. S. Bailey, for example, biblical hermeneutics began to interpret the Bible's prohibitions of same-sex relationships in the historical context of ancient cultures and times.[40] In his discussion of "How the Church Changed Its Mind" about homosexuality, Dr. Jack Rogers pointed to "a breakthrough in understanding the Word of God" as paving the way. This breakthrough in biblical interpretation urged Christians to read the Bible in a Christ-centered way and in the larger context of trying to answer pressing questions about the church's teaching on divorce and remarriage, race and civil rights, and the roles of women.[41]

As with the struggles for racial and gender equality, the strides that LGBTQ people made toward tolerance and inclusion were not uniform and came at the cost of significant controversy, struggle, animosity, and sometimes violence. Gay identity and liberation groups, some of which were formed as early as 1950, began to actively protest and press for their civil rights in the mid-1960s. The National Planning Conference of Homophile Organizations (NACHO), which met in Kansas City in 1966, was attended by representatives of fourteen separate groups. Adopting the slogan "Gay is Good," NACHO represented twenty-six gay rights organizations, and in 1968 NACHO published and popularized the "Homosexual Bill of Rights."[42]

Social advances often engender as much pushback as progress. For example, writing in *The Washington Post*, Emily S. Johnson recalled,

> By the late 1970s, gay rights groups were flourishing in the big centers of New York and San Francisco. . . . They had some success at winning inclusion in local anti-discrimination codes. These victories energized the movement, but they were deeply troubling to Christian conservatives, who approved of the pre-1960s status quo and the legal bans on homosexuality that reflected their moral values.[43]

This conservative pushback was epitomized, as both Hall and Johnson noted, by "the high-profile campaign" of singer, celebrity, and former Miss

39. Friedman and Downey, "Special Article," 923–30.

40. Bailey, *Homosexuality*.

41. Rogers, *Jesus, the Bible, and Homosexuality*, 35–51.

42. Andryszewski, *Gay Rights*, 12.

43. Johnson, "Myth That Has Shaped the Christian Right."

America Anita Bryant's attempt to halt the repeal of local sodomy laws. Bryant's efforts and others like them engendered controversy and conflict that conservative Christians, like "the Moral Majority," described as "culture wars."

The "culture wars" hit the recently formed UMC particularly hard because of Methodism's historic combination of *both* conservative and progressive elements; the traditional affirmation of "Scriptural Christianity" (Wesley's term) was, from the very outset, to be lived out in radical Christian discipleship that was often countercultural. Once again, as with the earlier controversies over race and gender, central components of the Wesleyan way of being Christian were pitted against each other, and Methodists of various persuasions and experiences soon found themselves taking positions on opposite sides of questions about the full inclusion of gay people in the life and ministries of the UMC. Nearly fifty years of passionate debate alienated many Methodists and caused significant departures of people on both sides of the question. The long controversy also made the UMC seem irrelevant and impotent at exactly the same time those indictments were being leveled at almost all "mainline" Protestants.

The current history of the UMC controversy over LGBTQ people is a complicated one that will be summarized here in broad terms by focusing upon several watershed events and policy decisions. Gay and lesbian UMC ministers struggled with whether to "come out" and expose themselves to trauma and potential retaliation, while others coped with unsettling news from loved ones who expressed a homosexual identity; both groups needed and deserved the support of their faith community. But for those less directly involved, it was easier to ignore the impending storm or maintain the *status quo*. In an attempt to begin to dispel misunderstanding and misinformation about gay people, UMC churches and church agencies addressed the dilemma through informational conferences, preaching, and other special events. One of the first of these events, held in May 1964, was a conference hosted by Glide Memorial UMC in San Francisco, where Rev. Cecil Williams led an effective ministry that included members of the gay community. As the gay rights movement developed, some UMC laity and clergy joined their struggle for tolerance and civil rights, while others opposed it. Caucuses and special interest groups began to form on both sides of the issue, with each trying to shape the conversations and to develop denominational policy that reflected their differing points of view.

In 1969, reacting to the Stonewall riots, the May issue of the UMC student magazine *Motive* generated significant controversy by including the concerns of lesbians in its support for women's rights and liberation. Criticism generated by this issue resulted in the UMC Board of Education temporarily halting the publication of *Motive*.[44] Following significant debate, in 1972, the same Board voted to defund the magazine. In apparent reply, the magazine's editorial page announced: "*Motive* Comes Out!" as it explored lives and spiritual experiences of lesbians,[45] and the final issue of *Motive* was devoted entirely to "Gay Men's Liberation."[46] About the same time, the public involvement of a few UMC clergy in the Gay Rights movement drew both support and criticism. In acts of protest, some ministers, like Gene Leggett of the East Texas Annual Conference, "came out" and were discontinued from clergy status. When *Life Magazine* featured an article on "Homosexuals in Revolt" in December 1971, it ran a photo of Rev. Leggett over the caption "Outcast Minister," and this catapulted the UMC's in-house controversy over the inclusion of queer people onto the national scene.[47]

Artist unknown, *Rev. Gene Leggett,* from the General Commission on Archives and History of the United Methodist Church, Madison, New Jersey, with permission.

The union of the EUB and the MEC in 1968 set in motion a review of the social principles for the new UMC. While both previous groups had a "Social Creed," neither of their creeds addressed the circumstances of LGBTQ people. The newly formed UMC appointed a study commission to update and develop new "Social Principles" and report back to the church at the 1972 General Conference. The commission's statement on gay people was, as described by Richey et al., a "pastoral statement [that] neither condemned nor condoned homosexual practice."[48] The Commission's two-sentence statement read:

> Homosexuals no less than heterosexuals are persons of sacred worth, who need the ministry and guidance of the church in their struggles for human fulfillment, as well as the spiritual and emotional support of a fellowship which enables reconciling relationships with God, with others and with themselves. Further we insist that homosexuals are entitled to have their human and civil rights ensured.[49]

44. "Dear Subscriber," 3.

45. "Motive Comes Out!" 1.

46. "Last Issue."

47. "Homosexuals in Revolt," 68.

48. Richey et al., *Methodist Experience*, 1:469.

49. Nickell, *We Shall Not Be Moved*, citing the *UMC Journal*, 1972, 1057, 95. See also McConkey, *United Methodists Divided*, 58.

The ensuing discussion featured many divergent voices on the issue; although a few delegates advocated the full inclusion of gay people, the predominant push from the floor of the General Conference (GC) was for stronger language directly condemning homosexual practice. After long and passionate debate, with motions, amendments, and counter-motions, the 1972 General Conference voted to add the statement "though we do not condone the practice of homosexuality and consider this practice incompatible with Christian teaching" to the end of the Commission's prepared paragraph. The amended statement affirmed the worth and personhood of gay people, while at the same time it condemned their authentic sexual self-expression.[50] This "solution" committed LGBTQ United Methodists to a bifurcated life that was both unacceptable and psychologically harmful to them.[51] Others argued that LGBTQ identity was not being condemned, but "homosexual *practice*" was; gay clergy and others could avoid ecclesiastical censure by remaining celibate (hence avoiding "fornication" for practicing sex outside of wedlock).

Since the 1972 General Conference, the UMC's position on the full inclusion of LGBTQ people has been discussed, studied, and debated at all levels of the church. In retrospect, these debates too often (in the words of an old adage) "generated more heat than light." Conservatives and traditionalists firmly believed that Scripture prohibits and condemns "homosexual practice" and felt they could not in good conscience move from that position. Liberals and progressives urged that any reading of Scripture that excluded and harmed people of faith could not be correct and urged Methodists to embrace their heritage of radical inclusion. The amount of pain, frustration, disillusionment, and disappointment these controversies produced is incalculable. The amount of time, spiritual energy, resources, and passion the controversy demanded, at the very time when the UMC was sliding into a deep decline in membership, vitality, and leadership in the world, must be lamented.

Polarization increased as special interest groups like "the Good News Movement" (1973) and the "UMC Gay Caucus" (1975) launched campaigns to win the church over to their point of view, and more often found themselves directly pitted against one another. The often rancorous debate was carried out in small groups, and on the floor of UMC Annual (AC) and General Conferences, even as the "Reconciling Congregations" sought to try to defuse homophobia through education and acts of reconciliation

50. Nickell, *We Shall Not Be Moved*, 96–102, 128–34, and Richey et al., *Methodist Experience*, I:469–71, both chronicled these developments.

51. Ford, "Coming Out," 93–110; Meyer, "Bias, Social Stress, and Mental Health," 674–97.

(1983). The net result of almost fifty years of conversations, study commissions, caucuses, proposals, and counterproposals can be summarized in six seemingly conflicting official statements from different parts of the UMC *Book of Discipline:*

> 1. All people are of sacred worth (para. 116G).
>
> 2. All people deserve equal rights (para. 162H).
>
> 3. Homosexual practice is not compatible with Christian teaching (para. 161F, 161G).
>
> 4. Pastors cannot officiate same-sex weddings (para. 332.6).
>
> 5. The church will not ordain self-avowed practicing homosexuals (para. 304.3).
>
> 6. Church agencies will not fund homosexual causes (para. 613, 806.9).[52]

For Methodists on both sides of the issue the tension caused by trying to live in the space between the church's "sacred worth" and "incompatible with Christian teaching" affirmations proved nearly impossible. It was particularly difficult for queer Methodists and for those whose loved ones lived within the boundaries of "sacred worth" and "incompatible." For others, the debate was still another example of the UMC forsaking biblical teaching to embrace popular culture. But for gay Methodists and their allies it felt like still another case of "justice delayed is justice denied."[53] Traditionalist Methodists, for whom the debate was often more theological or ideological than personal, drew a connection between the controversy and the institutional decline that was both deeply troubling and a source of ongoing frustration. *Good News* magazine, one of the voices of evangelical United Methodists, signaled its growing frustration when it changed its subtitle from: "A Forum for Scriptural Christianity *Within* the United Methodist Church," to "Leading United Methodists to a Faithful Future." The clear implication was that a "faithful future" might not be found "*within* the United Methodist Church."[54]

The *Book of Discipline's* (BOD) inclusion of the phraseology "of self-avowed, practicing homosexuals" as an attempt to try to forestall "witch-hunts" for LGBTQ clergy actually resulted in a disingenuous "don't ask, don't tell" (DADT) path to UMC clergy status that roughly paralleled the

---

52. See McConkey, *United Methodists Divided*, 11; see 10–20 for a helpful review of these statements.

53. King, "Letter from a Birmingham Jail." The maxim is said to have originated with British jurist William Gladstone, but that cannot be substantiated.

54. See *Good News Magazine*, at https://goodnewsmag.org/

position of the US military (especially from 1993–2011). As impatience and frustration regarding the UMC's position on LBGTQ people grew, so did acts of protest and disobedience, as partnered gay UMC clergy, like Rev. Rose Mary Denman, "came out" (1987). "'Self-avowed, practicing,' are the words that make a difference," Denman said. "If somebody says they're not practicing, they can stay in."[55] The conflict reached the point that Denman was no longer interested in remaining in the UMC *even if* the 1988 General Conference changed the ruling. "Just because the law is there doesn't mean you're accepted," she said, "I feel I'm too old to have to apologize for who I am."[56]

Concrete steps toward mutual understanding and reconciliation were sometimes taken, like the "Commission on the Study of Homosexuality" (1992), but those steps did not lead to a resolution. The diverse Commission of 1992 could *not* come to agreement on the main issues, but it was able to establish a consensus list of "Things the Church Can Responsibly Teach" regarding LGBTQ people, as well as "Things the Church Cannot Responsibly Teach." This consensus offered a foundation for further, substantive conversation. But it produced meager results when the 1992 GC received, but did *not* vote to approve, the commission's report. As a result, perhaps, the 1992 GC made changes in the BOD to support the civil rights of LGBTQ people, but no provision was made for a path toward reconciliation or greater harmony in the church about the full inclusion of LGBTQ people in the UMC.[57]

A second main point of conflict emerged when the UMC's prohibition of clergy officiating at same-sex marriages collided with legalization that recognized and legalized them in various states. Rev. Paul Abels, for example (1977),[58] and Rev. Jimmy Creech lost their ministerial standing for conducting same-sex marriages (1999).[59] The UMC refusal to allow clergy to bless same-sex unions became a sticking point in ecumenical conversations about "full communion" with other mainline Protestant denominations, like the Evangelical Lutheran Church of America.[60] UMC prohibition became increasingly difficult for some UMC American clergy when the US Supreme Court struck down all state laws banning same-sex marriage in

55. "Prohibition on Homosexual Ministers," 23.

56. "Prohibition on Homosexual Ministers," 23.

57. Oliverto, *Our Strangely Warmed Hearts*; Richey et al., *Methodist Experience*, II:670–71.

58. Richey et al., *Methodist Experience*, I:535; "Rev. Paul Abels."

59. Oliveto, *Our Strangely Warmed Hearts*, ch. 2.

60. "United Methodist Church to Consider."

2015, even though the UMC BOD prohibition against conducting same-sex weddings remained unchanged.

It was hoped that the 2016 GC would find a way to reconcile the opposing factions and iron out the ambiguities in the UMC BOD. After debates that the press characterized as "fierce and sometimes hurtful," the GC accepted a proposal from the UMC Council of Bishops that postponed a final decision until a "Group Discernment Process" was undertaken over the next four years. Building on the model of the early Methodist conferences, it was hoped that regional study groups could build the grass-roots consensus that seemed to be lacking throughout the UMC.[61] By a vote of 428 to 405, the "Discernment Process" proposal was adopted and a thirty-two member "Way Forward Commission" was charged with the responsibility of producing options for resolving the forty-four-year-long controversy. A "Special GC" session was scheduled for the Spring of 2019 for the church to receive the Commission's report and resolve the controversy. As Heather Hahn reported, "General Conference delegates have hit the pause button on the denomination's quadrennial debates related to homosexuality."[62] But to others, like Emma Green writing in *The Atlantic*, the "pause" looked a lot more like a "punt"—just kicking the problem further down the field.[63] In the meantime annual conferences and local congregations were urged to undertake a four-week study using the *Unity of the Church and Human Sexuality* curriculum provided by the General Board of Higher Education and Ministry.

During the 2016 GC "pause," acts of clerical disobedience and non-compliance with the UMC BOD continued. The most notable of these was the Western Jurisdictional Conference's unanimous eighty-eight-to-zero decision to elect a married lesbian UMC pastor, Rev. Karen Oliveto, to the office of bishop. On appeal the UMC Judicial Council offered "a somewhat muddled ruling," stating Rev. Oliveto was a duly elected bishop and therefore "remains in good standing," but that she also violated the UMC BOD as a "self-avowed practicing homosexual."[64] The council ruled that the matter of her violation of the BOD was not under its jurisdiction. In her autobiography, Bishop Oliveto recalled the painful "four decades" that the UMC spent treating gay people "as an issue to be resolved rather than [as] children

61. Hahn, "GC2016."

62. Hahn and Hodges, "GC2016 Puts Hold on Sexuality Debate."

63. Green, "Divided United Methodist Church."

64. Oliveto, *Our Strangely Warmed Hearts:* and Richey et al., *Methodist Experience*, II:670–71.

of God."[65] The Judicial Council's decision regarding her election caused strenuous reaction, and particularly from traditionalists, but was strangely reminiscent of their previous decision that argued that while female UMC clergy, like Dr. Georgia Harkness, were duly ordained by their annual conferences, they were not eligible for appointment as parish ministers. It was hoped that the Special GC of 2019 would bring resolution to the controversy over matters associated with the full inclusion of LGBTQ people in the UMC.

A second major event that took place during the 2016 "pause" was the establishment of the Wesleyan Covenant Association (WCA). WCA described itself as "an association or network of individuals and congregations who share a common understanding of our Wesleyan doctrine and desire to become a vibrant, faithful, growing, twenty-first-century church."[66] WCA was "to prepare for and live into a positive and faithful future."[67] In essence, this meant forming associations, coalitions, and alliances to help shepherd traditionalists and their goals through the upcoming GC and, if necessary, the formation of a new Methodist Church.

Photo by Mike Dubose, UM News, *Bishop Karen Oliveto,* **used with kind permission.**

As the Way Forward Commission did its work, three rather different proposals developed: 1) "The One Church Plan," which proposed that in order to keep the UMC united, the church should take no official position on matters like LGBTQ clergy and same-sex marriages, and allow those decisions to be made by conscience on a local level; 2) "The Connectional Conference Plan" postulated the creation of three "values-based" jurisdictions for traditionalist, centrist, or progressive United Methodists to replace the five regional jurisdictions already at work in the US; and 3) "The Traditional Plan," which proposed keeping the BOD prohibitions against LGBTQ people intact, and provided exit options for those who could not comply with them.[68] The Special GC was set for February 23–26, 2019, to hear and act upon the Way Forward Commission's report, as well as nearly a hundred related petitions and resolutions.

65. Oliveto, *Our Strangely Warmed Hearts*, sec. 2, introduction.

66. "About Us."

67. "About Us."

68. McConkey, *United Methodists Divided*, 134–47.

When the Way Forward Commission report came before the GC on February 26, 2019, the deliberations focused upon the "One Church Plan" and the "Traditional Plan." When the subsequent vote was taken, the "Traditional Plan" was adopted by 438 to 384. Since a recent poll of the US delegates indicated that two-thirds of them favored the "One Church Plan" that would likely avoid schism, it was assumed that delegates from Africa and churches beyond North America had swayed the results toward the Traditional Plan.[69] Kimberly Reisman, director of World Methodist Evangelism saw in the vote a seismic shift in the balance point of the Methodist family of churches: "It appears that we are now a more thoroughly global, evangelical church, rather than simply a mainline, American denomination with missionary outposts outside the US."[70] It seems sadly ironic that the full *inclusion* of Methodists from the non-Western churches resulted in the *exclusion* of queer people in North America! In view of the implications of the vote, the GC proposed developing a "gracious exit plan" for those who could not continue under the new regulations.

The Atlantic's headline read: "Conservative Christians Just Retook the United Methodist Church."[71] But what was heralded as a victory by some was for others a victory that felt more like a divorce or a funeral. "I think there's a lot of grief on all sides," said Keith Boyette, head of the WCA.[72] But the pain was much more personal for the members of the LBGTQ community: "We queer clergy begged our fellow Methodists to love us," wrote Rev. Hannah Adair Bonner of Tucson. "They voted no."[73] Rev. Adam Hamilton, a self-described centrist, believed the modified Traditional Plan was unacceptable to centrists and as well as progressives.[74] Calling themselves "UMC Next," Rev. Hamilton, along with Bishop Sue Hampert-Johnson, Rev. Junius Dotson, Bishop Mike McKee, and others, began a new church that adhered to "a Wesleyan vision of Christianity" and it sought to "to eliminate discriminatory language and the restrictions and penalties in the Discipline regarding LGBTQ persons. We affirm the sacred worth of LGBTQ persons, celebrate their gifts, and commit to being in ministry together."[75]

The 2019 GC directive to develop "a gracious exit plan" resulted in the formation of a representative sixteen-member mediation team that drafted

69. Steele, "United Methodists."

70. Steele, "United Methodists."

71. Green, "Conservative Christians," 1.

72. Green, "Conservative Christians," 3.

73. Bonner, "We Queer Clergy."

74. Green, "Conservative Christians," 3.

75. "Four Commitments of UMCNEXT."

an eight-page "Protocol of Reconciliation and Grace through Separation," which was slated for presentation and approval at the 2020 GC of the UMC. But the 2020 General Conference planned for May 5–15 in Minneapolis was postponed until August 2021 due to the onset of the coronavirus (COVID-19) pandemic, and consideration of the Protocol was forestalled. In his *Associated Press* article, David Crary wrote, "With split delayed, United Methodists face a year in limbo."[76] Crary's tacit assumption that the UMC split was delayed but not avoided was correct. The pandemic "pause" put the church's debate over its policy toward queer people on the backburner and forced a reexamination of how Methodists "do" church, but it did not resolve the controversial issues.

While diverse voices and viewpoints emerged during the reimagining of Methodism, at least three main factions were discernible. The conservatives, or traditionalists, represented by the WCA, supported the traditional BOD statements and prohibitions about same-sex relationships and accepted the Protocol as an opportunity to birth a new Methodist church that reflected their own views and values. The centrists, epitomized by UMC Next, advocated the full inclusion of LGBTQ people in the mission and life of the church and the acceptance of the Protocol as a way to end conflict by changing the current UMC *Discipline* to reflect their point of view. And a third group, the liberationists, represented by the "Out of Chaos" commission, believed that the Protocol of Reconciliation did not go far enough in remaking the church's priorities and processes to address the massive problems faced by millions of marginalized people all over the globe.[77] Recognizing "the pain and struggle" that characterize so many lives, they asked, "Might we imagine a United Methodist Church that empowers the disinherited and marginalized?"[78]

When the pandemic pause, intended to last one year, instead became one that lasted four years, frustration grew and the earlier consensus about the Protocol evaporated. Peter Smith, writing in *US News*, rightly described the devolution of the UMC as "a slow-motion schism."[79] "There's a lot that's happened since that protocol was signed, and the context has changed," Bishop Thomas Bickerton, president of the UMC Council of Bishops, explained.[80] More than 300 UMC congregations have already been approved

76. Crary, "With Split Delayed."

77. Astle, "'Out of Chaos,'" 2.

78. Astle, "'Out of Chaos,'" 3–4.

79. Smith, "United Methodists."

80. Miller, "What Happened?"

for separation, and an estimated 1,000 more applications are pending.[81] The salient developments that have moved the schism forward are the afore-mentioned loss of support for the Protocol and the establishment of the new Global Methodist Church (GMC) by the WCA and other conservative United Methodists.

The *Religion News Service* reported five of the people who had origi-nally negotiated and signed the original Protocol issued a statement report-ing that they "no longer in good faith" could support the plan or vote for its adoption at the upcoming UMC General Conference in September 2024.[82] The signatories opined, "The overwhelming consensus among those with whom we spoke is that the once-promising Protocol Agreement no longer offers a viable path forward, particularly given the long delays, the changing circumstances within the United Methodist Church, and the formal launch of the Global Methodist Church in May of this year."[83] Writing in *United Methodist Insight*, David Livingston described the May 7, 2022 launch of the Global Methodist Church (GMC) as "The Day the Protocol Died." "I have no doubt," Livingston opined, "that if we had held General Conference at the originally scheduled time in 2020 it would have passed."[84] While he had originally viewed the agreement as "the least bad option," Livingston wrote, "I'm nearly certain that it now has no chance of passing."[85]

With the launch of the GMC many more conservative congregations have begun the prescribed discernment process for disaffiliating from the UMC. It seems, however, some WCA congregations will stay on board the old ship long enough to pass the Protocol if they can. Writing on the new GMC website, for example, Rev. Keith Boyette reported: "We are confident Africa Initiative, Good News, the Confessing Movement, UMAction, and the Wesleyan Covenant Association will continue to vociferously advocate for the ultimate passage of the Protocol. Every theologically conservative local congregation and annual conference should have the right to join the Global Methodist Church with all of their property and assets intact."[86] The question that remains, then, is no long whether a schism will occur—since it has already begun—but whether the two opposing sides can agree to the

81. Smith, "United Methodists."

82. Miller, "What Happened?"

83. Miller, "What Happened?"

84. Livingston, "Day the Protocol Died."

85. Livingston, "Day the Protocol Died."

86. Global Methodist Church, "Global Methodist Church Sets Official Launch Date."

amicable divorce implied by passing "The Protocol of Reconciliation and Grace through Separation" at the 2024 UMC General Conference.

Did the separations that have led to schism have to happen? The answer is clearly "no." Once again, Methodist history reads like a litany of missed opportunities. Why did controversy over the UMC's full inclusion of LGBTQ people bring its fellowship to the breaking point? It looks like still another instance of Methodists losing sight of crucial elements of their vital heritage, or—perhaps better said—of losing the balance point between cherished Methodist verities. How could a choice between the Wesleys' "Scriptural Christianity" and their "Catholic Spirit" of inclusive Christian love ever be a satisfying or reasonable one for Methodists? And yet no workable consensus was built, and now both sides will lose something essential to being a vital Christian community—each other. Will fellowship among the new Methodist churches continue, despite institutional separations and divisions? Perhaps. However, the polarization and turf protection that led to the current crisis makes it seem unlikely. But out of death, Christians affirm, comes new life. As Methodists representing the various constituencies have said, hidden within the current painful schism may be an opportunity for building a new and productive future through rebirth, renewal, and reimaging of what it means to be a truly Christian church, in the Methodist mode.

FOR FURTHER CONSIDERATION:

1. Ultimately who gets to decide what the Bible means? How? Why? For whom?

2. To what extent is it incumbent upon you to allow your knowledge and religious views to be shaped or informed by contemporary culture? For good? For ill?

3. How much is your own point of reference on the inclusion of LGBTQ shaped by your own life experiences (or lack of them)?

4. In what ways did the bigness of the UMC "big tent" contribute to the growing polarization that accompanied this controversy? Could polarization have been avoided? How?

5. How do you decide whether a particular issue of Christian doctrine or practice is so significant that a disagreement about it must lead to separation and divisions among Christians?

Conclusion

WE HAVE COME TO the end of this narration of the Methodist family story. The Methodists have journeyed long and far from the London of 1738. We have been accompanied by "a great cloud of witness" (Heb 12:1–2) who have been Methodism's shapers and exemplars. They were people who followed Christ, in the Methodist mode, and set a high standard to which we may aspire, from which we might learn and which we can hope and pray to replicate. I hope that along the way you have found a few soulmates among our relatives, the faithful women and men, people like: Sarah Crosby and Mary Bosanquet Fletcher, Ann Oliver and Georgia Harkness, Francis Asbury and James O' Kelly, Nicholas Snethen and Orange Scott, Harry Hosier and Richard Allen, William McClain and Roy C. Nicholas, Marjorie Matthews and Karen Oliveto, and so many others who have contributed so much to who we are and what we have become.

Our forerunners have left us concrete examples of what it looks like to try to live out Mr. Wesley's mandate: "to spread Scriptural holiness across the land, beginning with the Church." Because of, and not in spite of, their deep love for the church, the Methodists tried to breathe new life into it; to pour new wine into old wine kins and to challenge the church's time-worn ways of doing things. Our forerunners embraced and tried to ameliorate the challenges that faced their church and nation with great compassion and incredible energy. The Methodists soon became a church, and then many churches, and as they did so they alleviated some institutional problems that plagued their predecessors but also created new ones. They continued to give themselves to helping the hopeless, poor, sick, hungry, excluded, oppressed, and marginalized people who were their neighbors. They understood their response as being endemic to their identity as Methodists and as faithful Christians.

Five years before his death, the elderly John Wesley mused about the future of the movement as he composed his "Thoughts Upon Methodism."

"I am not afraid," he wrote, "that the people called Methodists should ever cease to exist either in Europe or America. But I am afraid, lest they should only exist as a dead sect, having the *form* of religion without the *power*. And this will undoubtedly be the case, unless they hold fast both to the doctrine, spirit, and discipline with which they first set out."[1] Wesley's concern about having "the form without the power" of godliness, phraseology he borrowed from 2 Timothy 3:5, was a perennial one with the Wesleys. It was found in the self-reflection of their journals, it resounds in their sermons and hymns, and it was part of their critique of religion "as usual" in eighteenth-century England.[2] They were not interested in going through the motions of piety, and they knew that piety without the transforming power of God's grace and love is nothing but an empty shell.

Later in the same treatise, as John Wesley summarized his own understanding of what Methodism was all about, Wesley urged: "it is only plain, scriptural religion, guarded by a few prudential [wise] regulations. The essence of it is holiness of heart and life; the circumstantials all point to this. And so long as they are joined together in the people called Methodists, no weapon formed against them shall prosper."[3] Methodism without this "essence" would be like ancient Israel without the ark of the covenant, *Ichabod!* (Heb: "the glory has departed," 1 Sam 4:21–22), or more colorfully, as John Wesley explained: "if ever the essential parts should evaporate, what remains will be dung and dross."[4]

The earlier Methodist controversies were emotionally and spiritually challenging moral territory for them, but also for me, and perhaps for you as well. It was painful to see people of faith talk past each other, lose some of their love for each other, and act in ways that excluded others. It was sad to see Christian friends and partners in prayer become political opponents in the ecclesiastical arena. But some struggles, like trying to find the balance point between faith and good works, or their staunch advocacy for love-centered soteriology, as well as the struggle to figure out how to preach, teach, and live Christian perfection—while filled with contention—mattered so much because they were as basis spirited explorations of "essential parts" of Methodism. The debate over separation (or schism) was more difficult in this respect, because two genuine but opposing Methodist principles were at stake. The one was epitomized by John's desire to keep the movement

1. J. Wesley, "Thoughts Upon Methodism," in *Works* (1872), XIII:258.

2. See J. Wesley, *Sermons*; and J. Wesley, "Describing Formal Religion," in *Works* (1872), VII:188–90, and etc.

3. J. Wesley, "Thoughts Upon Methodism," in *Works* (1872), XIII:260.

4. J. Wesley, "Thoughts Upon Methodism," in *Works* (1872), XIII:260.

vital, and the other Charles's passion to keep it faithful. So it came down to a question of priorities: Which mattered most—and to whom? While not very spiritually satisfying, perhaps, looking at the debate is helpful because it helps us see that strong disagreements about principle will occur from time to time. These are often heated controversies because they involved important matters; but too often they seem to have (borrowing phrases from an old adage) generated "more heat than light."

The controversies over matters like women's leadership, the full inclusion of people of African descent, the laity, and LGBTQ people were rooted in principles vital to Methodism, but also became rancorous because the Methodists did not pass the test of their "three little rules," the first two being "do no harm," and "do all the good you can." The apparent, periodic absence of Mr. Wesley's famous "Catholic Spirit" among us calls into question our adherence to the third rule as well, our commitment to the practice of the Methodist "means of grace." Ours is a spirituality shaped by those holy practices, since this is where love for one another can be rekindled, and true fellowship can be restored. It is also helpful for us to recall that John Wesley, who coined the phrase "Catholic Spirit," and Charles Wesley, who sang its praises, also sometimes fell short of "Catholic love" toward each other and toward those with whom they strongly differed.

People have, can, and no doubt will continue to argue that the MEC's failures to practice its heritage of radical inclusion does not apply equally across the board when considering our record on gender, race, gender identity, and orientation. But I think those concerns do parallel each other. In each case the Methodist church chose the "safe road" of avoiding the potential conflict that would have come with full inclusion that was, at that time, based in controversial counter-cultural biblical social norms. In each case, however, they found or followed interpretive practices that also used the Bible to support or justify exclusionary actions, or an absence of difficult actions. And in each case, the Methodists forfeited the opportunity and obligation to provide moral leadership, apparently opting to follow repressive social trends instead.

The many missed opportunities to foster greater inclusion are as instructive as they are heart-breaking; why didn't Bishop Asbury ordain Harry Hosier? Why weren't the segregationist-minded trustees of St. George's Methodist Church remonstrated instead of Richard Allen? We have lost a long list of would-be reformers: James O' Kelly, Richard Allen, James Varick, Nicholas Snethen, Orange Scott, B. T. Roberts, Ann Howard Shaw, Margaret Newton Van Cott, Gene Leggett, Rose Mary Denman, and so many others. Why is it always the people who want or need change who so often wind up leaving our fellowship? Why have we been more patient with inequality than we have been ready for reform? And while women are finally more visible among us at various levels of leadership, most of our churches are still very monochromatic, and lay pastors—who serve mightily—do not vote on their own governance, and LGBTQ people continue to experience exclusion because of who they are or whom they love.

Do these apparent "failures" of our Catholic spirit evidence an evaporation of any of what Mr. Wesley described as Methodism's essential parts? Perhaps they do; and if they do, Wesley's assessment about what is left over stings as much as it stinks; "nothing but dung and dross," he wrote. In some instances, it seems we have kept the ecclesiastical body intact by giving up the spirit. But instead of shouting, "*Ichabod!* The glory has departed!" we would be better served by rekindling our first love, "holiness of heart and life," through the third of our "three simple rules"—"attend upon the means of grace." Through them, we can still find the "power of godliness" that the people called Methodists craved so deeply, and sought so ardently, so very long ago. It is a good time for us, borrowing Mr. Wesley's words, to try again "to reform the nation, beginning with the church"[5]—that is, beginning with ourselves.

5. J. Wesley, *Works* (1872), VIII:299.

Bibliography

Abbott, Susannah. "Clerical Responses to the Jacobite Rebellion in 1715." *Historical Research* 76.193 (August 2003) 332–46.

"About Us." *The Wesley Covenant Association*. http://wesleyancovenant.org/about.

Addison, Joseph. *The Spectator: A New Edition*. 8 vols. London: Routledge, 1891. https://www.gutenberg.org/ebooks/12030/.

Allen, J. Timothy. "'Some Expectation of Being Promoted'; Ambition, Abolition, and the Reverend James O'Kelly." *The North Carolina Historical Review* 84 (Jan 2007) 59–81.

Allen, Richard. *The Life Experiences and Gospel Labors of the Rt. Rev. Richard Allen*. Philadelphia: Lee & Yeocum, 1887.

Allestree, Richard. *The Whole Duty of Man Laid Down in a Plain and Familiar Way For the Use of All, But Especially the Meanest Reader, With Private Devotions For Several Occasions*. London: SPCK, 1658.

"Amendment VIII: Thomas Jefferson, A Bill for Proportioning Crimes and Punishments." *Founder's Documents*, Papers 2 (1778) 492–504. https://press-pubs. uchicago.edu/founders/documents/amendVIIIs10.html.

Andrews, Dee. *Methodists in Revolutionary America*. Princeton: Princeton University Press, 2000.

Andryszewski, Traci. *Gay Rights*. New York: Twenty-First Century, 2000.

Artlark. "Gay Georgian London: Horace Walpole amongst the 'Finger Twirlers.'" *Artlark*, September 24, 2022. http://artlark.org/2020/09/24/horace-walpole-gay-gentlemen-of-the-eighteenth-century.

Asal, Victor, and Udi Sommer. *Legal Path Dependence and the Long Arm of the Religious State: Sodomy Provisions and Gay Rights in Nations and Over Time*. New York: New York University Press, 2016.

Asbury, Francis. *The Causes, Evils, and Cures of Heart and Church Divisions: Extracted from the Works of Burroughs and Baxter*. New York: Lane & Scott, 1849.

———. *The Journal and Letters of Francis Asbury*. Edited by Elmer Clark. 3 vols. Nashville: Abingdon, 1958.

Astle, Cynthia B. "'Out of Chaos' to Create 'Vision Map' for Church." *United Methodist Insight*, December 1, 2020. https://um-insight.net/in-the-church/umc-future/ group-enters-second-round-of-envisioning-a-new-umc/.

Bailey, D. S. *Homosexuality and the Western Christian Tradition*. London: Longmans, 1955.

Baker, Frank. *John Wesley and the Church of England*. London: Epworth, 1970.

————, ed. *The Works of John Wesley.* Vol. 20, *Letters,* II. Oxford: Clarendon, 1982.

Bangs, Nathan. *The History of the Methodist Episcopal Church.* 4 vols. Cincinnati: Hitchock & Waldren, 1880.

————, ed. *The Life of the Rev. Freeborn Garrettson Compiled from His Printed and Manuscript Journals.* New York: T. Mason and G. Lane, 1838.

Berger, Teresa. "Charles Wesley and Roman Catholicism." In *Charles Wesley: Poet and Theologian,* edited by S. T. Kimbrough, 205–22. Nashville: Abingdon/Kingswood, 1992.

Black, John Bennett. *The Reign of Queen Elizabeth.* Oxford: Clarendon, 1959.

Blain, Keisha N. "Enslaved People in Eighteenth-Century Britain: An Interview with Nelson Mundell." *Black Perspectives* October 10, 2018. https://www.aaihs.org/enslaved-people-in-eighteenth-century-britain-an-interview-with-nelson-mundell/.

Blane, Rodney M. "Notes and Documents: Philip Thicknesse's Reminiscences of Early Georgia." *Georgia Historical Quarterly* 74 (Winter 1990) 672–98.

Boehm, Henry. *Reminiscences, Historical and Biographical, of Sixty Four Years in the Ministry.* New York: Carlton and Porter, 1868.

Bonner, Hannah Adair. "We Queer Clergy Begged Our Fellow Methodists to Love Us. They Voted No." *The Washington Post,* March 1, 2019. https://www.washingtonpost.com/outlook/queer-clergy-begged-our-fellow-methodists-to-love-us-they-voted-no/2019/03/01/ac1a232c-3b87-11e9-aaae-69364b2ed137_story.html.

The Book of Homilies: A Critical Edition. Edited by Gerald Bray. London: James Clarke and Co., 2015.

Boswell, James. *The Life of Samuel Johnson: Complete and Unabridged.* New York: Modern Library, 1936.

Boswell, John. *Christianity, Social Tolerance and Homosexuality.* Chicago: University of Chicago Press, 1980.

————. "The Church and the Homosexual: An Historical Perspective." Excerpts from his keynote address to The Fourth Biennial Dignity Convention, 1979. https://sourcebooks.fordham.edu/pwh/1979boswell.asp.

Brekus, Catherine A. "Female Preaching in Early Nineteenth-Century America." *The Center for Christian Ethics at Baylor University,* 20–29. https://www.baylor.edu/CONTENT/SERVICES/DOCUMENT.PHP/98759.PDF.

Brendlinger, Irv. *Social Justice through the Eyes of Wesley: John Wesley's Theological Challenge to Slavery.* Kitchener, ON: Joshua, 2006.

————. "Wesley, Whitefield, a Philadelphia Quaker, and Slavery." *Wesleyan Theological Journal* 36 (Fall 2001) 164–74.

Brine, M. E. "Burial in Woollen." *Devon Heritage,* July 31, 2009. http://www.devonheritage.org/Nonplace/Genealogy/BurialinWoollen.htm.

Butler, David. *Methodists and Papists: John Wesley and the Catholic Church in the Eighteenth Century.* London: Darton, Longman & Todd, 1995.

Byrne, Fone. *A Road to Stonewall: Male Homosexuality and Homophodia in English and American Literature, 1750–1969.* New York: Twayne, 1995.

Campbell, Ted. *John Wesley and Christian Antiquity.* Nashville: Kingswood, 1991.

————, ed. *The Works of John Wesley.* Vol. 27, *Letters III.* Nashville: Abingdon, 2015.

Canaday, Margot. "We Colonials: Sodomy Laws in America." *The Nation,* September 3, 2008. https://www.thenation.com/article/archive/we-colonials-sodomy-laws-america/.

Canny, Nicholas P. "The Ideology of English Colonization: From Ireland to America." *William and Mary Quarterly* 30 (Oct. 1973) 575–98.

Carter, Paul A. "The Negro and Methodist Union." *Church History* 21.1 (March 1952) 55–70.

Charleston, Libby-Jane. "The Truth Behind Queen Elizabeth's White 'Clown Face' Makeup." *Medium*, September 12, 2019. https://libbyjanecharleston.medium.com/the-truth-behind-queen-elizabeths-white-clown-face-makeup-c0507a178bd5.

Chilcote, Paul, ed. *Her Own Story: Autobiographical Portraits of Early Methodist Women*. Nashville: Abingdon, 2001.

———. *John Wesley and the Women Preachers of Early Methodism*. Lanham, MD: Scarecrow, 1991.

———, ed. *The Methodist Defense of Women in Ministry: A Documentary History*. Eugene, OR: Cascade, 2017.

———. *She Offered Them Christ: The Legacy of Women Preachers in Early Methodism*. 1993. Reprint, Eugene, OR: Wipf & Stock, 2001.

Church of England. *Catechism of the Church of England (1662)*. Edited by John Baskerville. Cambridge: Cambridge University Press, 1962.

Clark, Elmer. *The Journal and Letters of Francis Asbury*. 3 vols. Nashville: Abingdon, 1958.

Clarke, Adam. *Memoirs of the Wesley Family*. New York: Lane & Tippett, 1848.

Colhouer, T. H. *Sketches of the Founders of the Methodist Protestant Church*. Pittsburgh: MPC, 1880.

Compton, D'Lane R., et al. "Introduction Queer Work in a Straight Discipline." In *Other, Please Specify: Queer Methods in Theology*, edited by D'Lane R. Compton et al., 1–34. Oakland: University of California Press, 2018.

Corlet, Molly. "Between Colony and Metropole." In *Black British History: New Persepecives*, edited by Hakim Adi, 37–51. London: Zed, 2019.

Cornfield, P. J. "Class and Name and Number in Eighteenth-Century Britain. *History* 72.234 (Feb. 1987) 36–61.

Cragg, Gerald. *Reason and Authority in the Eighteenth Century*. Cambridge: Cambridge University Press, 1964.

———, ed. *The Works of John Wesley*. Vol. 11, *The Appeals to Men of Reason and Religion and Certain Related Open Letters*. Oxford: Clarendon, 1975.

Crary, David. "With Split Delayed, United Methodists Face a Year in Limbo. *AP News*, May 4, 2020. https://apnews.com/article/ap-top-news-reinventing-faith-marriage-mn-state-wire-virus-outbreak-457d5d0ec9218ac80c7b2497248d6b65.

Cruickshank, Joanna. *Pain, Passion and Faith: Revisiting the Place of Charles Wesley in Early Methodism*. Lanham, MD: Scarecrow, 2009.

Cugoano, Ottabah. *Thoughts and Sentiments on the Evil and Wicked Traffic of the Slavery and Commerce of the Human Species Humbly Submitted to the Inhabitants of Great-Britain, by Ottobah Cugoano a Native of Africa*. London: n.p., 1787.

Davies, Rupert, ed. *The Works of John Wesley*. Vol. 9, *The Methodist Societies*. Nashville: Abingdon, 1989.

Davis, Morris. "The Birth of a Nation, Birth of a Church." In *Christianity and the Politics of Race in the Jim Crow Era*, by Morris Davis, 23–44. New York: New York University Press, 2008.

Day, Felicity. "'A Nation Addicted to Gaming': The Georgian's Crackdown on Addictive Betting." *History Extra*, August 20, 2018. http://www.historyextra.com/period/georgian/gaming-gambling-betting-addiction-georgian-britain-games-cards/.

"Dear Subscriber." *Motive* XXX (July 7, 1969) 3. http://sth-archon.bu.edu/motive/issues/1969_May/assets/basic-html/page-3.html.

Defoe, Daniel. *Conjugal Lewdness, or Martimonial Whoredom*. London: T. Warner, 1727.

———. *Everybody's Business Is Nobody's Business: Or Private Abuses, Public Grievances, Exemplified in the Pride, Insolence, and Exhorbitant Wages of Our Women, Servants, and Footmen*. London: W. Meadows, 1725.

———. *The Great Law of Subordination Consider'd; Or the Insolence and Unsufferable Behavior of Servants in England Duly Enquir'd Into; Illustrated With a Great Variety of Examples, Historical Cases, and Remarkable Stories of the Behavior of Some Particular Servants . . . in Ten Letters*. London: S. Harding Lewis, 1724.

———. *The Shortest Way with the Dissenters or Proposals for the Establishment of the Church*. London: n.p., 1702.

———. *The True-Born English Man: A Satire*. Leeds, UK: Alice Mann, 1701.

Dillon, Frank. *Gin: The Much-Lamented Death of Madam Geneva*. Boston: Justin Charles, 2003.

Disraeli, Benjamin. *Sybil: The Two Nations*. 2 vols. London: Henry Colburn, 1845.

Donovan, Robert Kent. "The Military Origins of the Roman Catholic Relief Programme of 1778." *The Historical Journal* 28 (March 1985) 79–102.

Dryden, John. "Absalom and Achitophel (1681)." *Poetry Foundation*. https://www.poetryfoundation.org/poems/44172/absalom-and-achitophel.

Duekson, Darren, and John Richardson. "Learning from the 'Dones' and 'Nones.'" *Christian Leader,* March 1, 2019. https://christianleadermag.com/learning-from-the-dones-and-nones/.

Dyche, Thomas, and William Pardon. *New General English Dictionary*. London: Richard Ware, 1735.

Ecclestone, Edward. *Noah's Flood, or the Destruction of the World, An Opera*. London: M. Clark, 1679.

The Editors of Encyclopaedia Britannica. "Frances Willard." *Encyclopaedia Britannica*. https://www.britannica.com/biography/Frances-Willard.

Edwards, Maldwin. *After Wesley: A Study of the Social and Political Influence of Methodism in the Middle Period, 1791–1849*. London: Epworth, 1935.

Edwards, Paul. "The History of Black People in Britain." *History Today* 31.9 (Sept. 1981) http://www.historytoday.com/archive/history-black-people-britain.

Eldridge, Lisa. *Face Paint: The Story of Makeup*. New York: Abrams, 2015.

Ellis, John. "Pragmatic Radicals and Idealistic Conservatives: Methodist Liminality in the Revolutionary World." *Fides et Historica* 48.1 (Winter/Spring 2016) 1–31.

Emsley, Clive, et al. "Black Communities." *The Proceedings of the Old Bailey*, December 1, 2012. https://www.oldbaileyonline.org/static/Black.jsp.

Evans, Frederick. *The State of the Poor; or an History of the Labouring Class in England from the Conquest to the Present Day*. 3 vols. London: J. Davis, 1797.

Ferling, John. "Myths of the American Revolution." *Smithsonian Magazine*, January 2010. https://www.smithsonianmag.com/history/myths-of-the-american-revolution-10941835/.

Field, Clive. "Counting Religion in England and Wales: The Long Eighteenth Century, c. 1680–c. 1840." *Journal of Ecclesiastical History* 63 (Oct. 2012) 693–720. http://clivedfield.files.wordpress.com/2012/03/eighteenth-century-statistics-published.pdf.

———. "Eighteenth-Century Religious Statistics." *British Religion in Numbers,* September 21, 2012. http://www.brin.ac.uk/eighteenth-century-religious-statistics.

———. "A Schilling for Queen Elizabeth: The Era of State Regulation of the Church Attendance in England." *Journal of Church and State* 50.2 (Spring 2008) 243–53.

Fielding, Henry. *An Enquiry into the Causes of the Late Increase of Robbers, etc. With Some Proposals for Remedy this Growing Evil.* London: A. Millar, 1751.

Finke, Roger, and Rodney Stark. *The Churching of America, 1776–1850.* New Brunswick, NJ: Rutgers University Press, 2005.

Finney, Charles. *Lectures on Revivals of Religion.* Tappan, NJ: Fleming Revel, 1835.

Fisher, James. *The Westminster Assembly's Shorter Catechism Explained, by Way of Question and Answer.* 4th ed. Philadelphia: William Young, 1840.

Ford, V. E. "Coming Out as Lesbian or Gay: A Potential Precipitant of Crisis in Adolescence." In *Sexual Minorities: Discrimination, Challenges, and Development in America,* edited by M. K. Sullivan, 93–110. New York: Haworth Social Work Practice, 2003.

"Four Commitments of UMCNEXT." https://www.umcnextfl.org/.

Fraizer, Tony. "The Invention of Mungo: Race and Representation in the Eighteenth-Century Atlantic World." *International Journal of the Arts and Humanities* 5.2 (April 2019) 17–27.

Franklin, John Hope. "Birth of a Nation: Propaganda as History." *The Massachusetts Review* 20.3 (Fall 1979) 430–31.

French, G. S. "Ruckle, Barbara (Heck)." In *Dictionary of Canadian Biography,* Vol. 5 (1801–1820), edited by James Nicholson. 22 vols. Toronto: University of Toronto Press, 1983. http://www.biographi.ca/en/bio/ruckle_barbara_5E.html.

Friedman, Richard C., and Jennifer Downey. "Special Article: Homosexuality." *The New England Journal of Medicine* 331 (Oct. 6, 1994) 923–30.

Fryer, Peter. *Staying Power: The History of Black People in Britain.* London: Pluto, 2018.

Gagnon, Robert. *The Bible and Homosexual Practice.* Nashville: Abingdon, 2002.

Gates, Henry Louis. *The Trials of Phillis Wheatley.* New York: Basic Civitas, 2003.

Gee, Joshua. *The Trade and Navigation of Great-Britain Considered.* London: Samuel Buckley, 1729.

"The General Rules of the Methodist Church." *The United Methodist Church,* 2016. https://www.umc.org/en/content/the-general-rules-of-the-methodist-church.

George, Dorothy. *England in Transition.* Baltimore: Penguin, 1953.

Georgian, Elizabeth A. "A Church in Crisis? Paradoxes in the Rise of American Methodism, 1777–1838." PhD diss., University of Delaware, 2010.

———. "That Unhappy Division: Reconsidering the Causes and Significance of the O'Kelly Schism in the Methodist Episcopal Church." *The Virginia Magazine of History and Biography* 120 (Fall 2012) 210–35.

Gerard, Kent, and Gert Heckma, eds. *The Pursuit of Sodomy: Male Homosexuality in Renaissance and Enlightenment Europe.* New York: Harrington Park, 1989.

Gerzina, Gretchen Holbrook. *Black London.* New Brunswick, NJ: Rutgers University Press, 1995.

"Getting the Vote." *National Museum of American History, Behring Center*, n.d. http://www.americanhistory.si.edu/democracy-exhibition/vote-voice/getting-vote.

Gifford, Carolyn DeSwarte. "'My Own Methodist Hive,' Frances Willard's Faith as Disclosed in Her Journal, 1855–1870." In *Spirituality and Social Responsibility*, edited by Rosemary Skinner Keller, 81–99. Nashville: Abingdon, 1993.

Gilbert, Alan. *Religion and Society in Industrial England: Church, Chapel, and Social Change*. London: Longman, 1976.

Gillard, Derek. *Education in England: A History*. Education in England, May 2018. www.educationengland.org.uk/history/chapter05.html.

Gillies, John, ed. *Memoirs of Rev. George Whitefield*. Middleton, MA: Hunt & Noyes, 1829.

Gleckner, Robert. *Gray Agonistes*. Baltimore: Johns Hopkins University Press, 1997.

Global Methodist Church. "Global Methodist Church Sets Official Launch Date." March 3, 2022. https://globalmethodist.org/global-methodist-church-sets-official-launch-date/.

Goldenberg, David. *Black and Slave: The History of the Curse of Ham*. Berlin: DeGruyter, 2017.

Gother, John. *A Papist Misrepresented and Represented*. London: James Marcus Corker, 1683.

Green, Emma. "Conservative Christians Just Retook the United Methodist Church." *The Atlantic*, Februaruy 26, 2019. https://www.theatlantic.com/politics/archive/2019/02/united-methodists-fracture-lgbt-plan-rejected/583693/.

———. "The Divided United Methodist Church." *The Atlantic*, May 18, 2016. https://www.theatlantic.com/politics/archive/2016/05/divided-methodist-church-lgbt/483396/.

Griffin, Marvin. *Latitudinarianism in the 17th Century of England*. London: Brill, 1992.

Grubb, Farley. "The Fatherless and Friendless: Factors Influencing the Flow of English Emigrant Servants." *The Journal of Economic History* 52.1 (March 1992) 85–108.

Hahn, Heather. "GC2016: The Debate about How to Debate Sexuality." *UM News*, April 15, 2016. https://www.umnews.org/en/news/gc2016-the-debate-about-how-to-debate-sexuality.

Hahn, Heather, and Sam Hodges. "GC2016 Puts Hold on Sexuality Debate." *UM News*, May 18, 2016. http://www.umnews.org/en/news/bishops-ask-for-hold-on-sexuality-debate.

Hamilton, Carol V. "Why Did Jefferson Change 'Property' to the 'Pursuit of Happiness?'" *History News Network*, January 27, 2008. https://historynewsnetwork.org/article/46460.

Harrington, Susan. "Friendship under Fire." *Andover Newton Quarterly* 15 (Jan. 1975) 167–81.

Harrington, William Holden. *John Wesley in Company with High Churchmen*. London: Church, 1870.

Harvey, Karen. "The Century of Sex." *The Historical Journal* 45 (Fall 2002) 899–916.

Hatch, Nathan. *The Democratization of American Christianity*. New Haven: Yale University Press, 1989.

Haynes, Clare. "The Culture of Judgment: Art and Anti-Catholicism in England, c. 1660–1760." *Historical Research* 78 (Nov. 2005) 483–505.

Hays, Richard B. "The Biblical Witness Concerning Homosexuality." In *Staying the Course*, edited by Maxie Dunnam and Dewton Maloney, 65–85. Nashville: Abingdon, 2003.

Heales, Alfred. *The History and Law of Church Seats or Pews*. 2 vols. London: Butterworths, 1872.

Heitzenrater, Richard. *Wesley and the People Called Methodists*. Nashville: Abingdon, 2013.

Higgenbotham, Peter. "Education in the Workhouse." *The Workhouse*, 2021. http://www.workhouses.org.uk/education/workhouse.shtml.

Hill, Harvey. "The Law of Nature Revived: Christianity and Natural Religion in the Sermons of John Tillotson." *Journal of Anglican and Episcopal History* 70.2 (June 2001) 169–89.

History.com Editors. "Stonewall Riots." *History.com*, May 31, 2017. http://www.history.com/topics/gay-rights/the-stonewall-riots.

Hitchcock, Tim, et al. "A Population History of London, 1674–1715." *The Proceedings of the Old Bailey*. https://www.oldbaileyonline.org/static/Population-history-of-london.jsp#a1674-1715.

———. "Workhouses." *London Lives, 1690 to 1800*. http://londonlives.org/static/Workhouses.jsp.

Hoeveler, Diane. "Anti-Catholicism and the Gothic Imagery: The Historical and Literary Contexts." In *Religion in the Age of Enlightenment*, edited by Brett C. McInelly, 1–35. New York: AMS, 2013.

"Homosexuals in Revolt." *Life Magazine* 71.26 (Dec. 31, 1971) 62–73. https://books.google.com/books?id=8z8EAAAAMBAJ&printsec=frontcover&source=gbs_ge_summary_r&cad=0#v=onepage&q&f=false.

Houghton, S. M., ed. *George Whitefield's Letters*. Edinburgh: Banner of Truth, 1976.

Hudson, Chuck. "Pastimes in the Georgian Era." *The Historic Interpreter*, November 11, 2014. http://historicinterpreter.wordpress.com/2014/11/11/entertainment-in-the-georgian-era.

Hume, David. "Of National Characters." In *Essays and Treatises on Several Subjects*, 119–28. London: T. Cadell, 1777.

Hurst, John Fletcher. *The History of British Methodism*. 7 vols. London: Eaton & Mains, 1904.

Irons, Kenda Weddle. "From Kansas to the World: M. Madeline Southard, Activist and Pastor." *Methodist History* 43.1 (Oct. 2004) 35–36.

Jackson, Francis, ed. *An Index to the Memoirs, Obituary Notices, and Recent Deaths, Together with the References to the Local Histories of Methodism*. Westcliff-on-sea, UK: Gage Postal, 1985.

Jackson, Thomas. *The Life of Charles Wesley, A.M.* New York: Lane & Sandford, 1842.

———. *The Lives of Early Methodist Preachers*. 6 vols. London: Wesleyan Methodist Book-Room, n.d.

Jennings, David. *A Vindication of the Scripture-Doctrine of Original Sin*. London: R. Hett, 1740.

Jenys, Soame. *Free Inquiry into the Nature and the Origin of Evil: In Six Letters*. London: R. J. Dolney, 1758.

Job, Rueben. *Three Simple Rules: A Wesleyan Way of Living*. Nashville: Abingdon, 2007. See also a study guide for small groups, by Jeanne Terance Finley, *Three Simple Rules for Christian Living*. Nashville: Abingdon, 2008.

Johnson, Emily. "The Myth That Has Shaped the Christian Right and the LGBTQ Rights Movement for Four Decades." *The Washington Post*, June 21, 2019. https://www.washingtonpost.com/outlook/2019/06/21/myth-that-has-shaped-christian-right-lgbtq-rights-movement-four-decades/

Johnson, Samuel. "London: A Poem in Imitation of the Third Satire of Juvenal." *Representative Poetry Online*, 2008. https://rpo.library.utoronto.ca/content/london-poem-imitation-third-satire-juvenal.

Jones, Brad A. "'In Favor of Popery': Patriotism, Protestantism, and the Gordon Riots in the Revolutionary British Atlantic." *Journal of British Studies* 52.1 (Jan. 2013) 79–102.

Jones, Major. "The Central Jurisdiction: Passive Resistance." In *Heritage and Hope: The African American Presence in United Methodism*, edited by Grant S. Shockley, 189–209. Nashville: Abingdon, 1991.

Jones, Pip, and Rita Youseph. *The Black Population of Bristol in the Eighteenth Century*. Bristol, UK: University of Bristol Press, 1994.

Keller, Rosemary Skinner. *Georgia Harkness: For Such a Time as This*. Nashville: Abingdon, 1992.

"Key Dates in Census, Staistics and Registration, Great Britain, 1000–1899." http://www.thepotteries.org/dates/census.htm.

Kilham, Alexander. *An Account of the Trial of Alexander Kilham, Methodist Preacher, Before the General Conference in London . . . Written by Himself*. Nottingham, UK: C. Sutton, 1796.

Kimbrough, S. T. "Charles Wesley and a Window to the East." In *Charles Wesley: Life, Literature and Legacy*, edited by Ted Campbell and Kenneth Newport, 165–83. Peterborough, UK: Epworth, 2007.

King, Martin Luther. "Interview on 'Meet the Press.'" *The Martin Luther King, Jr. Papers Project*, April 17, 1960. http://okra.stanford.edu/transcription/document_images/Vol05Scans/17Apr1960_InterviewonMeetthePress.pdf.

———. "Letter from a Birmingham Jail." *University of Pennsylvania, African Studies Center*, April 16, 1963. https://www.africa.upenn.edu/Articles_Gen/Letter_Birmingham.html.

———. *Why We Can't Wait*. New York: Harper & Row, 1964.

King, Peter, and John Carter. "Black People and the Criminal Justice System: Prejudice and Practice in Later Eighteenth and Early Nineteenth Century London." *Historical Research* 88.239 (February 2015) 100–124.

Klein, Lawrence. "Gender and the Public/Private Distinctions in the Eighteenth Century." *Eighteenth Century Studies* 19.4 (Fall 1995) 97–109.

Knight, Jude. "The Rakehell in Fact and Fiction." *Dirty Sexy History*, October 27, 2016. https://dirtysexyhistory.com/2016/10/27/the-rakehell-in-fact-and-fiction/.

Laqueur, Thomas. *Making Sex: Body and Gender from the Greeks to Freud*. Cambridge: Harvard University Press, 1990.

Laqueur, W. T. *Religion and Respectability: Sunday Schools and Working Class Culture*. New Haven: Yale University Press, 1976.

"Last Issue." *Motive* XXXII.2 (1972). http://sth-archon.bu.edu/motive/issues/1972_GayMensLiberation/assets/basic-html/page-1.html. (This link no longer works.)

"Latitudinarian." *The Episcopal Church*. https://www.episcopalchurch.org/glossary/latitudinarian-latitudinarianism/.

Lavington, George. *The Enthusiasm of Methodists and Papists Comp'd.* London: J. and P. Knapton, 1754.

"The Law In England, 1290–1885." *Fordham University.* https://sourcebooks.fordham.edu/pwh/englaw.asp.

Lee, Benjamin Franklin, ed. "Harry Hosier and Richard Allen." *The Christian Recorder,* Philadelphia, PA, May 13, 1886.

Lee, Jesse. *A Short History of the Methodists in the United States of America.* Baltimore: Magill and Clime, 1810.

Leger, J. A. *John Wesley's Last Love.* London: J. M. Dent, 1910.

Lein, Clayton D. "Jonathan Swift and the Population of Ireland." *Eighteenth Century Studies* 8 (Summer 1975) 431–53.

Livingston, David. "The Day the Protocol Died." *United Methodist Insight,* May 16, 2022. https://um-insight.net/in-the-church/umc-future/the-day-the-protocol-died/.

Lloyd, Gareth. *Charles Wesley and the Struggle for Methodist Identity.* Oxford: Oxford University Press, 2007.

———. "'A Cloud of Perfect Witnesses': John Wesley and the London Disturbances 1760–1763." *The Asbury Theological Journal* 57 (Fall 2001, Spring 2002) 117–36.

———. "'Running After Strange Women': An Insight into John Wesley's Troubled Marriage from a Newly Discovered Manuscript Written by His Wife." *Proceedings of the Wesley Historical Society* 53 (May 2002) 169–74.

———. "Sarah Perrin (1721–1787): Early Methodist Exhorter." *Methodist History* 41.2 (April 2003) 79–88.

Lobody, Diane. "A Wren Just Bursting Its Shell: Catherine Livingston Garrettson's Ministry of Public Domesticity." In *Spirituality and Social Responsibility,* edited by Rosemary Keller, 19–40. Nashville: Abingdon, 1993.

Locke, John. *An Essay Concerning Human Understanding.* Edited by Peter H. Nidditch. Oxford: Clarendon, 1979.

Lyles, Albert M. *Methodism Mocked.* London: Epworth, 1960.

MacClenny, W. E. *Life of O'Kelly and the Early History of the Christian Church in the South: A Restorationist Movement Biography.* Raleigh: Edwards and Broughton, 1910.

Madan, Martin. *Thoughts on Executive Justice With Respect to Our Criminal Law: With Respect to Our Criminal Laws, Particular on the Circuits.* London: J. Dodsley, 1785.

Maddock, Ian. "Solving a Transatlantic Puzzle? John Wesley, George Whitefield, and 'Free Grace' Indeed." *Wesley and Methodist Studies* 8 (Jan. 2016) 1–15.

Maddox, Randy, and Timothy Underhill. "Untangling the Tangled Web: Charles Wesley and Elizabeth Story." *Wesley and Methodist Studies* 6.2 (2016) 175–83.

Magennis, Eoins. "The Present State of Ireland, 1749." *Irish Historical Studies* 36 (Nov. 2009) 581–97.

Mandeville, Bernard. *The Fable of the Bees, or Private Vices, Public Benefits.* (1732). https://www.earlymoderntexts.com/assets/pdfs/mandeville1732_1.pdf.

"Margaret Newton Van Cott." *The United Methodist Church Archives and History.* http://www.gcah.org/history/biographies/margaret-newton-van-cott.

Maser, Frederick. *Seven Sisters in Search of Love.* Rutland, VT: Academy, 1988.

Mathews, Donald G. *Methodism and Slavery: A Chapter in American Morality, 1780–1845.* Princeton: Princeton University Press, 2016.

Mathias, Peter. "The Social Structure of the Eighteenth Century: A Calculation by Joseph Massie." *Economic History Review* X (1958) 30–45.

McClain, William B. "Black People in the Methodist Church: A Fierce Fidelity to a Church for Whom Grace Is Central." *Methodist History* 54.1 (Oct. 2015) 81–92.

———. *Black People in the Methodist Church: Whither Thou Goest?* Nashville: Abingdon, 1984.

McConkey, Dale. *United Methodists Divided.* Rome, GA: Global Parish, 2018.

McInerney, Timothy. "The Better Sort: Nobility and Human Variety in Eighteenth Century Great Britain." *Eighteenth Century Studies* 38.1 (March 2015) 47–63.

McNeil, Peter. *Pretty Gentlemen.* New Haven: Yale University Press, 2018.

Medley, Yvonne J. "Racism Influences Methodist History." *The United Methodist Church.* archives.umc.org/interor.asp?/mid=664. (This link no longer works.)

"Methodist Church in Ireland: History." Methodist Church in Ireland. https://www.irishmethodist.org/our-history.

Meyer, I. H. "Bias, Social Stress, and Mental Health in Lesbian, Gay, and Bisexual Populations: Conceptual Issues and Research Evidence." *Psychological Bulletin* 129.5 (2003) 674–97.

Miller, Emily McFarlan. "What Happened to United Methodists' Proposal to Split the Denomination?" *Religion News Service*, June 29, 2022. https://religionnews.com/2022/06/29/what-happened-to-united-methodists-proposal-to-split-the-denomination/.

Molineaux, Catherine. "Hogarth's Fashionable Slaves: Moral Corruption in Eighteenth-Century London." *English Literary History* 72 (Summer 2005) 47–53.

Montagu, Mary Wortley. *Letters from the Right Honourable Lady Mary Wortley Montagu.* Edited by R. Brunly Johnson. London: J. M. Dent, 1906.

Moore, Arthur Allen, III. "Catherine 'Kitty' Livingston Garrettson." *Find a Grave*, February 15, 2010. https://www.findagrave.com/memorial/48178792/catherine-garrettson.

Morgan, Edmund S. "The Puritans and Sex." *The New England Quarterly* 15.4 (Dec. 1942) 591–607.

Morgan, William Thomas. "An Eighteenth-Century Election in England." *Political Science Quarterly* 1 (Dec. 1922) 580–95.

"Motive Comes Out!" *Motive* XXXII.1 (1972). http://sth-archon.bu.edu/motive/issues/1972_LesbianFeminist/assets/basic-html/page-3.html. (This link no longer works.)

Myers, Robert Manson. "Mrs. Delany: An Eighteenth-Century Handelian." *Musical Quarterly* 32.1 (1946) 12–36.

Nelson, James. *An Essay on the Government of Children: Under Three General Heads, viz. Health, Manners, and Education,* London: R. and J. Dodsely, 1763.

Neuburg, Victor E. *Popular Education in Eighteenth-Century England.* London: Woburn, 1971.

Newman, Richard S. *Freedom's Prophet: Bishop Richard Allen, the AME Church, and the Black Founding Fathers.* New York: New York University Press, 2008.

Newport, Kenneth, ed. *The Sermons of Charles Wesley: A Critical Edition with Introduction and Notes.* Oxford: Oxford University Press, 2001.

Nickell, Jane Ellen. *We Shall Not Be Moved: Methodists Debate Race, Gender, and Homosexuality.* Eugene, OR: Pickwick, 2014.

Nind, John Newton. *Mary Clark Nind and Her Work: By Her Children.* Chicago: Methodist Mission Society, 1906.

"Noble Savage." *Encyclopedia Britannica*. https://www.britannica.com/art/noble-savage.

North, Eric. *Early Methodist Philanthropy*. New York: Methodist Book Concern, 1914.

Norton, Rictor. "The Macaroni Club: Homosexual Scandals in 1772." *Homosexuality in Eighteenth-Century England*, December 19, 2004. http://rictornorton.co.uk/eighteen/macaroni.htm.

―――. *Mother Clap's Molly House: The Gay Subculture in England 1700–1830*. London: GMP, 1992. https://rictornorton.co.uk/molly.htm.

―――. "Newspaper Reports, 1721–1723." *Homosexuality in Eighteenth-Century England*, March 3, 2004. http://rictornorton.co.uk/eighteen/1721news.htm.

Norwood, Frederick. *The Story of American Methodism*. Nashville: Abingdon, 1974.

O'Brien, George. *An Economic History of Ireland in the Eighteenth Century*. London: Maunse, 1918.

O'Brien, Richard Barry. *Studies in the History of Ireland, 1649–1775*. London: MacMillian, 1903.

O'Kelly, James. *Author's Apology for Protesting Against the Methodist Episcopal Government*. Hillsbourgh, UK: Dennis Heartt, 1829.

Oliverto, Karen. *Our Strangely Warmed Hearts: Coming Out into God's Call*. Nashville: Abingdon, 2018.

Orwell, George. *England, Your England*. New York: Penguin, 1982.

Outler, Albert. *Theology in the Wesleyan Spirit*. Nashville: Tidings, 1975.

Parker, Richard, ed. *The Private Journal and Literary Remains of John Byrom*. 2 vols. Manchester: Chetham Society, 1888.

Parratt, Catriona. "Robert W. Malcolmson's 'Popular Recreations in English Society, 1700–1850,' an Appreciation." *Journal of Sport History* 29 (Summer 2002) 312–23.

Payne, Dianne. "London's Charity School Children: The 'Scum of the Parish?'" *British Journal for Eighteenth-Century Studies* 29 (2006) 383–97.

Pelikan, Jaroslav, ed. *Luther's Works*. Vol 3, *Lectures on Genesis 15–20*. St. Louis: Concordia, 1961.

Perkin, Harold. *The Origins of Modern English Society*. London: Routlege, 1969.

Petrie, Charles. *The Four Georges: A Revaluation of the Period From 1714–1830*. London: Eyre & Spottswoode, 1935.

Podmore, Colin. *The Moravian Church in England: 1728–1760*. Oxford: Clarendon, 1998.

Pope, Alexander. "The Essay on Man." In *An Essay on Man: Moral Essays and Satires*, edited by Henry Morley. London: Cassels, 1891. https://www.gutenberg.org/files/2428/2428-h/2428-h.htm.

Porter, Roy. *English Society in the Eighteenth Century*. London: Penguin, 1982.

"Prohibition on Homosexual Ministers Faces a Test." *The New York Times*, July 5, 1987. https://www.nytimes.com/1987/07/05/us/prohibition-on-homosexual-ministers-faces-a-test.html.

Rack, Henry. "'But Lord, Let It Be Betsy!' Love in Early Methodism." *Proceedings of the Wesley Historical Society* 53 (Feb. 2001) 1–13.

―――. *Reasonable Enthusiast: John Wesley and the Rise of Methodism*. Philadelphia: Trinity, 1989.

―――, ed. *The Works of John Wesley*. Vol. 10, *Methodist Societies, the Minutes of Conference*. 54 vols. Nashville: Abingdon, 2011.

Rattenbury, John. *The Evangelical Doctrines of Charles Wesley's Hymns.* London: Epworth, 1941.

"Resolution on Appropriate Affirmative Responses to Sexual Orientation Distress and Change Efforts." *American Psychological Association,* August 2009. https://www. apa.org/about/policy/sexual-orientation.

"Rev. Paul Abels, 54, First Openly Gay Minister." *Chicago Tribune,* March 15, 1992. http://www.chicagotribune.com/news/ct-xpm-1992-03-15-9201240301-story. html.

Richardson, Harry V. "Early Black Methodist Preachers." *Journal of the Interdenominational Theological Center* 3.1 (Fall 1975) 11–21.

Richey, Russell, et al. *The Methodist Experience in America.* 2 vols. Nashville: Abingdon, 2000.

Roberts, Mary Lee A., and Martin Schiavenato. "Othering in the Nursing Context: A Concept Analysis." *National Library of Medicine* 4.3 (2017) 174–81. https://www. ncbi.nlm.nih.gov/pmc/articles/PMC5500989/.

Rogers, Jack. *Jesus, the Bible, and Homosexuality.* Louisville: Westminster John Knox, 2009.

Rogers, Nicholas. "Popular Protest in Early Hanoverian London." *The Past and Present Society* (May 1979) 70–100.

Ross, David, ed. "Henry VIII's 1534 Act of Supremacy (1534)." *Britain Express.* https:// www.britainexpress.com/History/tudor/supremacy-henry-text.htm.

Rowe, Kenneth E. "Evangelism and Social Reform in the Pastoral Ministry of Anna Oliver." In *Spirituality and Social Responsibility,* edited by Rosemary Skinner Keller, 117–38. Nashville: Abingdon, 1993.

Salmon, D. "Work of the Charity Schools." In *The Encyclopedia and Dictionary of Education,* edited by Foster Watson, 294–95. London: Pittman and Sons, 1921.

Sancho, Ignatius. *Letters of the Late Ignatius Sancho, an African.* Edited by Joseph Jerkyll. 2 vols. London: J. Nicholas, 1782.

Sandhu, Sukhdev. "The First Black Britons." *BBC,* February 17, 2011. www.bbc.co.uk/ history/british/empire_seapower/black_britons_01.shtml.

Sandys, George. *A Relation of a Journey Begun An. Dom. 1610.* London: W. Barrett, 1615.

"Sarah Crosby Woman Preacher." *The Asbury Triptych Series.* https://www. francisasburytriptych.com/sarah-crosby-woman-preacher.

Schiesbinger, Londa. "The Anatomy of Differences: Race and Sex in Eighteenth-Century Science." *Eighteenth-Century Studies* 23 (Summer 1990) 385–405.

Schlenther, Boyd S. "Whitefield, George, 1714–1770." *Oxford Dictionary of National Biography,* September 23, 2004. https://doi.org/10.1093/ref:odnb/29281.

Scott, Orange. *An Appeal to the Methodist Episcopal Church.* Boston: David Ela Printer, 1838.

Scroggs, Robin. *The New Testament and Homosexuality.* Philadelphia: Fortress, 1983.

Segal, David. "That Diss Song Known as 'Yankee Doodle." *The New York Times,* July 1, 2017. https://www.nytimes.com/2017/07/01/sunday-review/that-diss-song-known-as-yankee-doodle.html.

Shaw, Anna Howard. *The Story of a Pioneer.* New York: Harper, 1915.

Sherwin, Oscar. "Crime and Punishment in England of the Eighteenth Century." *The American Journal of Economics and Sociology* V.2 (Jan. 1946) 169–99.

Shipley, Joseph. *The Origins of English Words: A Discursive Dictionary of Indo-European Root*. Baltimore: Johns Hopkins University Press, 1984.

Shockley, Grant S. "The Methodist Episcopal Church: Promise and Peril." In *Heritage and Hope: The African American Presence in United Methodism*, edited by Grant S. Shockley, 39–99. Nashville: Abingdon, 1991.

Shoemaker, Robert. B. "The London 'Mob' in the Early Eighteenth Century." *Journal of British Studies* 25.3 (July 1987) 273–304.

Simpson, Matthew, ed. *Cyclopedia of Methodism*. Philadelphia: Louis Everts, 1880.

Sledge, Robert W. "A Step Back or a Step Forward? The Creation of the Central Jurisdiction." *Methodist History* 34.1 (Oct. 2015) 10–22.

Small, Stephen. "Reconstructing the Black Past." *Albion* 29 (Winter 1997) 689–91.

Smith, John Q. "Occupational Groups among the Early Methodists Keightley Circuit." *Church History* 57.2 (June 1988) 187–96.

Smith, Mark. *Secular Faith: How Culture Has Trumped Religion in American Politics*. Chicago: University of Chicago Press, 2015.

Smith, Peter. "United Methodists Are Breaking Up in a Slow-Motion Schism." *US News*, October 10, 2022. https://www.usnews.com/news/us/articles/2022-10-10/united-methodists-are-breaking-up-in-a-slow-motion-schism.

Smith, Timothy L. *Revivalism and Social Reform: American Protestantism on the Eve of the Civil War*. Eugene, OR: Wipf & Stock, 2004.

Smith, Warren Thomas. *Harry Hosier: Circuit Rider*. Nashville: Upper Room, 1981.

Snethen, Nicholas. *Lay Representation; or Essay on Lay Representation and Church Government, Collected from the Wesleyan Repository, Mutual Rights, and The Mutual Rights and Christian Intelligencer, from 1820 to 1829 Inclusive, and Now Republished in a Chronological Order, with an Introduction by the Rev. Nicholas Snethen*. Baltimore: J. J. Harrod, 1835.

———. *A Reply to an Apology for Protesting Against the Methodist Episcopal Government*. Philadelphia: Henry Tuckness, 1800.

Solomonson, Lesley Jacobs, ed. *Gin: A Global History*. London: Reakton, 2012.

South, Robert. *Twelve Sermons and Discourses on Several Subjects and Occasions*. London: Jonah Rowyer, 1717.

Southern, R. W. *St. Anselm: A Portrait in Landscape*. Cambridge: Cambridge University Press, 1990.

Stanton, Elizabeth Cady, ed. *History of Women's Suffrage*. 4 vols. New York: Fowler & Wells, 1881.

Steele, Anthony. *History of Methodism*. London: George Vickers, 1857.

Steele, Jeremy. "Steinberg, Jessica. *Seven Deadly Sins of Prostitution: Perceptions of Prostitutes in Eighteenth-Century London*. Ottawa: University of Ottawa Press, 2015.

———. "United Methodists Vote to Keep Traditional Marriage Stance." *Christianity Today*, February 26, 2019. https://www.christianitytoday.com/news/2019/february/united-methodist-lgbt-vote-conference-plan.html.

Stetzer, Ed. "If It Doesn't Stem Its Decline, Mainline Protestantism Has Just 23 Easters Left." *Washington Post*, April 28, 2017. https://www.washingtonpost.com/news/acts-of-faith/wp/2017/04/28/if-it-doesnt-stem-its-decline-mainline-protestantism-has-just-23-easters-left.

Stone, Lawrence. *The Family, Sex, and Marriage in England, 1500–1800*. New York: Harper and Row, 1971.

————. "Literacy, and Education in England, 1640–1900." *Past and Present* 42 (1969) 69–139.

Straker, Ian B. "Black and White and Gray All Over: Freeborn Garrettson and African American Methodism." *Methodist History* 37.1 (Oct. 1998) 18–27.

Sugden, Edward. "A Wesley Class Register." *Proceedings of the Wesley Historical Society* XII (Dec. 1919) 75–77.

Swift, Jonathan. "*Baucis* and *Philemon*." *Eighteenth-Century Poetry Archive*. https://www.eighteenthcenturypoetry.org/works/psw11-w0060.shtml.

————. *Miscellanies*. London: John Morphew, 1713.

————. *The Present Miserable State of Ireland*. Cork, Ireland: CELT (Corpus of Electronic Texts): A Project of University College Cork, 2008. https://celt.ucc.ie//published/E700001-010.html.

Sykes, Norman. *Church and State in England in the 18th Century*. Hamden, CT: Archon, 1962.

Szreter, Simon, and Kevin Sierna. "The Pox in Boswell's London: An Estimate of the Extent of Syphilis Infection in the Metropolis in the 1770s." *Economic History Review* 74.2 (May 2021) 372–99.

Talley, Colin. "Gender and Male Same-Sex Erotic Behavior in British North America in the Seventeenth Century." *Journal of the History of Sexuality* 6 (Jan. 1966) 305–408.

Taylor, John James. "Church and State in England in the Mid-Eighteenth Century." PhD diss., Jesus College, Cambridge University, 1987.

Telford, John. *Two West-End Chapels, or Sketches of London Methodism from Wesley's Day*. London: Epworth, 1886.

Thom, Danielle. "Sawney's Defence: Anti-Catholicism, Consumption, and Performance in 18th Century Britain." *V&A Online Journal* 7 (Summer 2015). http://www.vam.ac.uk/content/journals/research-journal/issue-no.-7-autumn-2015/sawneys-defence-anti-catholicism,-consumption-and-performance-in-18th-century-britain/.

Thomas, J. D. "The Case of Somersett from Freedom's Journal." *Accessible Archives*, November 30, 2012. https://www.accessible-archives.com/2012/11/case-of-somersett-from-freedoms-journal/.

Tillotson, John. *The Works of the Rev. Dr. John Tillotson, Lord Archbishop of Canterbury*. 12 vols. London: R. Wade, 1743.

Townsly, Jeremy. "Queer Sects in Patristic Commentaries on Romans 1:26–27, Goddess Cults, Free Will, and Sex Contrary to Nature." *Journal of the American Academy of Religion* 81.1 (March 2013) 56–79.

Trusler, John. *Three Short Letters to the People of England, Proving the Public Grievances Complained of to Be Ideal*. London: n.p., 1790. https://quod.lib.umich.edu/cgi/t/text/text-idx?c=ecco;idno=004862597.0001.000.

Tucker, Robert Leonard. *The Separation of the Methodists from the Church of England*. New York: The Methodist Book Concern, 1918.

Tyerman, Luke. *The Life of Rev. George Whtiefield*. 2 vols. London: Hodder & Stoughton, 1876.

Tyson, John R. *Assist Me to Proclaim: The Life and Hymns of Charles Wesley*. Grand Rapids: Eerdmans, 2007.

————. "Charles Wesley and the Church of England: A Commemorative Essay." *Anglican and Episcopal History* 76.4 (Dec. 2007) 464–88.

————, ed. *Charles Wesley: A Reader*. Oxford: Oxford University Press, 1989.

———. "Charles Wesley, Evangelist: The Unpublished New Castle Journal." *Methodist History* 25 (Oct. 1986) 41–61.

———. *Charles Wesley on Sanctification.* Grand Rapids: Zondervan, 1986.

———. *The Great Athanasius: An Introduction to His Life and Work.* Eugene, OR: Cascade, 2017.

———. "An Instrument for Sally: Charles Wesley's Shorthand Biography of John Davis." *Methodist History* XXX.2 (January 1991) 103–8.

———. "Lady Huntingdon, Religion, and Race." *Methodist History* 50 (Oct. 2011) 28–40.

———. "A Poor, Vile Sinner: Lady Huntingdon's Language of Weakness and Deference." *Methodist History* 37.2 (Jan. 1991) 107–19.

———. "Why Did John Wesley Fail? A Reappraisal of Wesley's Evangelical Economics." *Methodist History* XXV.3 (Apr. 1997) 176–88.

Tyson, John R., and Boyd S. Schlenther, eds. *In the Midst of Early Methodism: Lady Huntingdon and Her Correspondence.* Lantham, MD: Scarecrow, 2006.

Tyson, John R., and Douglas Lister. "Charles Wesley Pastor: A Glimpse Inside His Shorthand Journal." *Methodist Quarterly Review* 4 (Spring 1984) 9–22.

United Methodist Church. *The Book of Discipline.* Nashville: United Methodist, 2016.

"United Methodist Church to Consider Full Communion with ELCA." *Evangelical Lutheran Church in America,* April 21, 2008. https://www.elca.org/News-and-Events/6149.

Vickers, Jason E. *Wesley: A Guide for the Perplexed.* London: T. & T. Clark, 2009.

Villarreal, Daniel. "Sodomy Laws Are Still Being Used to Harass LGBT People." *LGBTQ Nation,* September 8, 2019. https://www.lgbtqnation.com/2019/09/sodomy-laws-still-used-harass-lgbtq-people/.

Voth, Hans-Jochim. "Time and Work in Eighteenth-Century London." *The Journal of Economic History* 58.1 (Mar. 1998) 29–58.

Walsh, John. "Methodism and the Mob in the Eighteenth Century." *Studies in Church History* 8 (1972) 213–27.

———. "Methodism at the End of the Eighteenth Century." In *A History of the Methodist Church in Great Britain,* edited by Rupert E. Davies and Gordon Rupp, 1:275–315. 4 vols. London: Epworth, 1965.

Walsh, Patrick. "A New Edmund Burke Letter from 1778." *Eighteenth-Century Ireland* 24 (2009) 159–63.

Waters, Michael. "The Macaroni in 'Yankee Doodle' Is Not What You Think." *Atlas Obscura,* August 24, 2016. http://www.atlasobscura.com/articles/the-macaroni-in-yankee-doodle-is-not-what-you-think.

Ward, Reginald. *The Protestant Evangelical Awakening.* Cambridge: Cambridge University Press, 1992.

Warrick, Susan. "'She Diligently Followed Every Good Work': Mary Mason and the New York Female Missionary Society." *Methodist History* 34.4 (July 1996) 214–29.

Welter, Barbara. "The Cult of True Womanhood." *American Quarterly* 18.2 (Summer 1966) 151–74.

Wesley, Charles. *Hymns for Those That Seek and Those That Have Redemption in the Blood of Jesus Christ.* London: Strahan, 1747.

———. *The Journal of Charles Wesley.* 2 vols. Edited by Thomas Jackson. London: Wesleyan Conference, 1849.

———. *The Letters of Charles Wesley*. Edited by Kenneth Newport and Gareth Lloyd. Oxford: Oxford University Press, 2013.

———. *The Manuscript Journal of the Reverend Charles Wesley, M. A.* Edited by Kenneth Newport et al. 2 vols. Nashville: Abingdon, 2007.

———. *Ms. Luke*, 232. https://divinity.duke.edu/initiatives/cswt/charles-manuscript-verse.

———. *The Representative Verse of Charles Wesley*. Edited by Frank Baker. Nashville: Abingdon, 1962.

———. *The Sermons of Charles Wesley: A Critical Edition with Introduction and Notes*. Edited by Kenneth Newport. Oxford: Oxford University Press, 2001.

———. *The Unpublished Poetry of Charles Wesley*. Edited by S. T. Kimbrough and Oliver Beckerlegge. 3 vols. Nashville: Abingdon, 1990.

Wesley, Charles, and John Wesley. *The Poetical Works of John and Charles Wesley*. Edited by George Osborn. 13 vols. London: Wesleyan Conference, 1886.

Wesley, John, ed. *The Christian Library: Extracts from and Abridgments of the Choicest Pieces of Practical Divinity Which Have Been Published in the English Tongue*. 50 vols. London: Dutton, 1821.

———. *Explanatory Notes Upon the Old and New Testament*. 4 vols. Salem, OH: Schmul, 1755.

———. *Journal and Diaries*. Edited by W. Reginald Ward and Richard P. Heitzenrater. 6 vols. Nashville: Abingdon, 1988–2003.

———. *The Journal of Rev. John Wesley A. M.* Edited by Nehemiah Curnock. 8 vols. London: Richard Culley, 1910.

———. *The Letters of the Rev. John Wesley*. Edited by John Telford. 8 vols. London: Epworth, 1931.

———. *Sermons*. Edited by Albert Outler. 4 vols. Nashville: Abingdon, 1987.

———. *The Works of John Wesley*. Edited by Thomas Jackson. 14 vols. London: Wesleyan Conference, 1872.

———. *The Works of John Wesley*. Vol. 7, *A Collection of Hymns for the Use of the People Called Methodists*. Edited by Franz Hilderbrandt and Oliver Beckerlegge. Nashville: Abingdon, 1989.

———. *The Works of John Wesley*. Vol. 12, *Doctrinal and Controversial Treatises I*. Edited by Randy Maddox. Nashville: Abingdon, 2012.

———. *The Works of John Wesley*. Vol. 13, *Doctrinal and Controversial Treatises II*. Edited by Paul Chilcote and Kenneth Collins. Nashville: Abingdon, 2013.

Wesley, Susanna. *The Complete Writings*. Edited by Charles Wallace. Oxford: Oxford University Press, 1997.

West, Cornel, ed. *The Radical King*. Boston: Beacon, 2015.

White, Jonathan. "The 'Slow But Sure Poyson,' the Representation of Gin and Its Drinkers." *Journal of British Studies* 42.1 (Jan. 2003) 35–64.

Whitefield, George. *George Whitefield's Journals*. London: Banner of Truth Trust, 1960.

———. *A Letter to the Rev. Mr. John Wesley. Occasioned by His Sermon against Predestination*. Pensacola, FL: Chapel Library, 1999. https://quod.lib.umich.e/evans/N03787.0001.001/1:4?rgn=div1;view=fulltext.

———. *The Works of the Rev. George Whitefield, M. A.* 4 vols. London: Dilly, 1771.

Whiteley, John. *Wesley's England*. London: Epworth, 1938.

Whittier, John Greenleaf. "Snow-Bound: A Winter Idyl." *The Poetry Foundation*. https://www.poetryfoundation.org/poems/45490/snow-bound-a-winter-idyl.

"Who Were the Black Loyalists?" *Black Loyalist Heritage Centre, part of the Nova Scotia Museum,* 2001. https://novascotia.ca/museum/blackloyalists/who.htm.

Wigger, John. *American Saint: Francis Asbury and the Methodists.* Oxford: Oxford University Press, 2009.

Wilder, Franklin. *The Methodist Riots.* New York: Todd & Honeywell, 1981.

Wiles, R. M. "Middle Class Literacy in Eighteenth Century England." In *Studies in the 18th Century,* edited by R. F. Brissenden, 49–67. Toronto: University of Toronto Press, 1968.

Willard, Frances. *Glimpses of Fifty Years: The Autobiography of an American Woman.* Chicago: B. J. Smith, 1889.

Willis, Andre C. "The Impact of David Hume's Thought about Race for the Stance on Slavery and His Concept of Religion." *Hume Studies* 42 (Apr/Sept 2016) 213–30.

Wilson, Thomas. *Distilled Spirituous Liquors: The Bane of the Nation.* London: J. Roberts, 1736.

Wink, Walter. *Homosexuality and the Bible.* New York: Fellowship, 1997.

Names and Subjects Index

Ancient Documents Index